MARTY LIQUORI'S

HOME GYM WORKOUT

MARTY LIQUORI'S
HOME GYM WORKOUT

MARTY LIQUORI and
GERALD SECOR COUZENS

BANTAM BOOKS
TORONTO • NEW YORK • LONDON • SYDNEY • AUCKLAND

MARTY LIQUORI'S HOME GYM WORKOUT
A Bantam Book / June 1986

Principal photography by Allen Cheuvront.
Equipment photographs provided by the manufacturer.

Library of Congress Cataloging-in-Publication Data

Liquori, Marty.
  Marty Liquori's home gym workout.
  1. Exercise 2. Exercise—Equipment and supplies.
3. Physical fitness. I. Couzens, Gerald Secor.
II. Title. III. Title: Home gym workout.
GV481.L643 1986   613.7'028   85–48110

ISBN 0-553-34257-6

Published simultaneously in the United States and Canada

PRINTED IN THE UNITED STATES OF AMERICA

RAND   0 9 8 7 6 5 4 3 2 1

Acknowledgments

PREPARING THIS BOOK WAS A MONUMENTAL TASK THAT WAS MADE much easier through the assistance, guidance, and contributions of many people. Paul Byrne was outstanding in his insightful perceptions of the home fitness industry and his knowledge about the workings of all the home machinery. He also reviewed the text and made important recommendations. Barry Lynn and Patricia Ripley, fitness consultants, were helpful with their suggestions. Many athletes and coaches offered their personal workouts using the different pieces of home equipment, and we're extremely grateful to them. They include John Howard, Peter Gardener, Bill Koch, and Dr. Larry Klecatsky. Phil Dunphy and his wife, Pat, directors of the H.E.A.R. Institute in Red Bank, New Jersey, gave us many hours of their time, making suggestions and offering their personal insights into home fitness and health. Bruria Ginton, massage therapist extraordinaire, reviewed the self-massage chapter and made important recommendations. Bruce Baltz was helpful in providing details about personal trainers. Allen Cheuvront, our chief photographer for the project, put in marathon shooting sessions and learned something about fitness as well.

Writing a book is more than just typing and submitting a manuscript. Much time, thought, and effort go on behind the scenes in getting out the final copy. Coleen O'Shea, our talented editor, is most responsible for this. She kept the book focused and gently prodded us to finish the book before the equipment became outdated. Jim Trupin, marathon runner, literary agent, and friend, kept close tabs on our work and equipment and is now curator of the Zen Home Workout Room. And special thanks to our wives and families, who supported us through the months of testing and writing.

Marty Liquori
Gerald Secor Couzens

The following quality home-fitness-equipment manufacturers were helpful in providing information about their products:

Amerec Corporation
AMF American
Computer Instruments Corporation
Concept II, Inc.
Cybex
Engineering Dynamics Corporation
Hooker Performance
Houdaille Industries
Ivanko Barbell Company
J. Øglænd, Inc.
Landice Products Corporation
M & R Industries, Inc.
Ogden Health Products
Paramount Fitness Equipment Corporation
Precor USA
PSI NordicTrack
Racer-Mate
Spenco Medical Corporation
Sportech, Inc.
Trotter Treadmills, Inc.
Universal Gym Equipment Company
West Bend
York Barbell Company, Inc.

Contents

PART I

MY HOME GYM

1   No Place Like Home   1

2   Home Sweet Home   8

3   The Ten Commandments
of Home Gym Workouts   15

PART II

HOME GYM EQUIPMENT & WORKOUTS

4   Stationary Bikes   51

5   Weight Training   83

6   Rowing Machines   117

7   Treadmills   141

8   Cross-Country Skiing   167

9   Heart-Rate Monitors   183

PART III
HOW TO HELP YOURSELF

10   Where to Shop   193

11   Massage   196

12   Do You Need a
Personal Trainer?   205

13   Injuries   208

Afterword   221

PART I

MY HOME GYM

ONE

NO PLACE LIKE HOME

I HAVE EXERCISED ALMOST EVERY DAY OF MY LIFE SINCE I STARTED running competitively when I was thirteen years old. And, from ages seventeen to thirty-one, I worked out twice a day preparing for major races in this country and around the world. During those years I read everything I could about athletic research and sports performance, and I tried almost every piece of exercise equipment in an effort to get the most out of my body and my training. Whenever I was injured and couldn't train, I devised my own workout routines to do in a pool or on a bicycle.

My persistence and dedication paid off. Running for Villanova University from 1967 to 1972, I won the NCAA mile title three times, the IC4A mile title six times, and helped Villanova win nine of nine races at the Penn Relays. In 1969 and again in 1977 I was ranked by *Track and Field News* magazine as the top 1,500-meter runner in the world, with best times of 3:37:2 and 3:36 respectively. Also in 1977 I was the top 5,000-meter runner in the world, with a best time of 13:15:1, an American record for the next five years. My best mile time was 3:52:2.

Since retiring from the international running circuit in 1980 soon after President Jimmy Carter refused to allow American athletes to participate in the 1980 Olympics in Moscow, I have confined my exercise workouts to my home gym. Here, I work not on running skills exclusively, but on total body conditioning. Although I no longer strive to be the fastest runner in the world, I still want to remain as fit as I can be. Weight work several times a week gives me my strength and body toning, while varied routines on my exercise bike, treadmill, cross-country ski machine, and rower provide the all-important aerobic exercise that strengthens my heart and lungs.

Although I was once a world-class runner, the purpose of this book

Beating Jim Ryun to the tape in one of our one mile duels. Photo credit: Rich Clarkson

is not to turn you into a competitive runner. Rather, I want to offer you a series of ability-based aerobic workouts that are designed to help you achieve your optimum physical fitness using exercise equipment designed specifically for use in the home. The workouts here include many of my favorites that I do every week. Others were recommended to me by coaches and Olympic and world-class athletes. As you will see, except for the weight workouts, all the exercises are aerobic. This means that the workout will demand that you breathe large quantities of oxygen for prolonged periods of time, and because of this, directly bring about substantial positive changes to the lungs and heart.

The word *aerobic* and the concept of strengthening the heart muscle above all others was first made popular in the 1960s by Dr. Kenneth Cooper, director of the Aerobics Center in Dallas. Dr. Cooper and most other physicians are in agreement that an aerobic exercise such as rowing, running, cross-country skiing, or cycling that is done for at least 20 to 45 minutes 3 times a week will help improve your cardiovascular system, lower your levels of anxiety and stress, and make you more fit and able to meet life's daily demands. I agree wholeheartedly with that assessment and make it a point to exercise at least 3 times a week using a variety of home exercise machines, training at a heart rate of at least 60 percent of my maximum heart rate for 20 uninterrupted minutes at a time.

In my athletic career I was fortunate to have had some of the best coaches in the world to advise me, most notably Fred Dwyer, my high school track coach at Essex Catholic H.S., now head coach at Manhattan College, and Jumbo Jim Elliot, my track coach and mentor at Villanova University. I have also learned a lot on my own from my years of sports training. On my shelf at home I have a collection of training diaries spanning my active running career. Noted inside are workouts—hard ones, easy ones, in-between ones—along with comments on my feelings and observations on what effect it had on me that particular day. I know what exercise has done for me and I know what it can do for you. In this book I will explain how you can integrate exercise into your life and how it can be done painlessly, interestingly, methodically, economically, and with the most positive health benefits. And this is something new in the realm of exercise: I will also explain how you can do it all in the privacy of your own home.

I have never considered myself an exercise evangelist or workout guru. However, I firmly believe that exercise, home exercise especially, can have a positive influence on your life. If you were to ask me to try to convince you that you need exercise, I'd be as excited as Picasso would have been to paint your garage. But ask me what to look for in quality home exercise equipment and how to get the most out of your home workouts every day, and I'll talk your head off.

Working out at home is becoming more and more commonplace in the United States, and I'm happy to see that happening. The fast pace of our lives and the demands of family and daily work cut deeply into whatever free time we have each day. Regular exercise is very often neglected in this rush. But now, with the advent of reliable, affordable, and compact home exercise equipment you can exercise in the privacy of your bedroom, cellar, or garage, or wherever you have the space. Of course, these machines can't sweat for you or provide you with the necessary willpower to continue with your exercise program, but they do offer the means to safely and efficiently achieve aerobic conditioning, strength, and flexibility.

In the past I listened quietly as health and fitness experts explained that if you want to get in shape all you have to do is go outside and run, ride your bike, or swim. Some of these experts even recommended gardening as a good form of exercise. Exercise machines to work out indoors? Just costly gimmicks for the weak-minded, said many of these experts.

But do these experts know something that I don't? No, I really don't think so. After almost two decades of training outdoors, and now after six years of exercising indoors in my own home gym, my retort is one based on my personal experience. How can you go out for a run if you get home late from work, there's a blizzard raging outside, and the temperature is too cold for even a polar bear? You can't!

How can you ride your bike outside in these same awful conditions? Or when it's ninety degrees with just as high humidity? Impossible!

And if you don't know how to swim or have access to a pool or some other body of water, your swimming program is sunk. As for gardening, if you have to wait until the spring thaw before you can get your gardening exercise, there's little value in it. For any exercise program to succeed it must be done on a regular, sustained basis. And this is something that the detractors of home exercise often conveniently fail to mention.

Working out in your home gym is the only sensible solution for someone looking for year-round exercise. Working out at home is not only more convenient but, more important, it's a much more sensible and efficient use of your time. With good equipment installed in your own exercise room (or even your bedroom!) you can cut away time lost in commuting to your local park or health club. Working out in your home gym also eliminates the time once spent waiting in long lines to use equipment.

Quality. Efficiency. Safety. These are the basic themes of this book. For all of you who want to work out efficiently and in a manner that will stand the test of time, read this book and learn. You will find out what features to look for when you're ready to buy a quality rower, treadmill, exercise bike, cross-country ski machine, or multistation weight machine. In addition to the health and fitness tips, there are also challenging workouts here at beginner, intermediate, and advanced levels that will help you to safely achieve your fitness goals.

Motivation—Dedication—Hard Work

Exercise isn't always easy. And working out at home, where the scenery is always the same, can become monotonous. But this doesn't mean that home exercise can't be interesting and fun. I'm sure that many of you are thinking that because I was once the world's best miler I am some sort of naturally gifted athlete who doesn't get bored, who doesn't sweat, feel fatigue, or get searing lungs during particularly difficult workouts. I do. All top athletes do. All beginning exercisers do. But what

Although I started my athletic career as a distance runner, I now work out on a variety of home exercise equipment.

keeps me going, what might separate me from other home exercisers, is the degree of my motivation and my intensity.

Motivation and intensity are intangibles that most people don't understand and never will. After seventeen years at the top as a runner and thirteen years working for ABC-TV as a commentator, I've learned a lot about both intensity and motivation. I've been fortunate to have met many of the world's top athletes. What has struck me most about each of them is their strong motivation to succeed in their sport and their extreme dedication to their training. Often, though, I've found that when the general public, bombarded by the media with only the trappings of success, sees a smiling Carl Lewis, or Mark Spitz, or Eric Heiden with Olympic medals draped around their neck, the response normally is, "It must have been easy for them. They're just naturally talented."

The main point that most people fail to understand is actually how hard these athletes had to work to achieve their goals. It's not natural talent or luck that gets these athletes to the top. It's motivation and the willingness to put in thousands of hours of training time.

Although you may never become an Olympic-caliber athlete, you still need some degree of motivation in order to achieve your goals, whatever they may be. This goes for everything you do, from moving up in your job to succeeding in your home exercise program. Successful people are those who focus on a goal and then deliberately set out a course to achieve their ambition. So you have great athletes in the history of sport like Mark Spitz, who swam five hours a day, or Eric Heiden, who skated for three hours a day, working on form and technique.

It's not that these Olympic medal winners are lucky or that they are natural athletes. No, their talent wasn't that they were Supermen or that they were seven feet tall, weighed 250 pounds, and bullied their way to the top by force of sheer size. No, their talent was simply that early on in their lives they discovered how to motivate themselves.

Spitz, Heiden, and Lewis, like all successful athletes, business people, artists, or musicians, are like torpedoes with self-controlling mechanisms. If they get blown off course, they correct themselves and get back on target. This is the illustration Maxwell Maltz used in his best-selling book, *Psycho-Cybernetics*. The human mind, says Maltz, is a torpedo, and if you have a goal that is strong enough, nothing will be able to get in your way (for long) to keep you from achieving that goal.

When I speak before business groups around the country I very often use the following example as an illustration to dispel the myth concerning the role of luck or natural talent as determining factors of success: A lady, an amateur musician herself, was deeply moved by a violinist at a Carnegie Hall recital one night. Once the concert ended, she rushed backstage to congratulate the violinist. "Maestro," she said, "I'd give half my life to play as beautifully as you did tonight." The violinist was silent for a moment, then said to her, "Madam, I already have."

My point is this: If you want to succeed at something, home exercise in this particular case, you have to set your mind to it. You must figure out what your goals are, plan your program, and then take the necessary steps to achieve your goals. Like the violinist at Carnegie Hall, luck or natural talent has little to do with your success. I learned that from my running career. Success, I've found out, takes motivation, dedication, and plenty of hard work.

TWO

HOME SWEET HOME

I STARTED MY HOME GYM WORKOUTS BECAUSE I WAS ANNOYED about a television sports show. Let me explain.

For years ABC-TV aired the Superstars, a made-for-TV event that pits athletes from football, soccer, basketball, baseball, boxing, hockey, and track against one another in a series of events including tennis, bicycling, rowing, bowling, sprinting, and navigating an obstacle course. All of this is done in an effort to find out which person is actually the best all-around athlete.

I was intrigued by the Superstars because, in essence, you had to be a classical athlete, one who was well versed, talented, coordinated, and strong enough to do well in a variety of sports.

I had always wanted to take part in the Superstars, particularly as I watched runner after distance runner falter when they went head to head with athletes from other sports. I was not naïve enough to think that I, a 6-foot, 143-pound distance runner could compete on an all-around level with the best from the NFL, NBA, or NHL. But I did feel that with some intelligent preparation I could do well. In 1981, with a scant two months' notice, I was invited to compete and I gladly accepted.

I started training twice daily. No, I didn't incorporate running as part of my training. Heresy, you must be thinking. But actually my goal was balanced over-all fitness. I wanted to shore up my weaknesses and spend only a little time working on my strengths. Running wasn't one of my weaknesses. But my years of running, with its overemphasis on the leg muscles, certainly left my body weak in a lot of other areas.

To achieve my aims and efficiently maximize what time I had for training, I went to the local sporting goods store in Gainesville, Florida, where I live, and bought exercise equipment specifically designed for home use. A thousand dollars later, my new home gym included a multistation weight machine, 200 pounds of free weights and dumbbells, a stationary bike, and a rowing machine. All of this new equipment fit neatly in my 20 x 30 exercise room off my living room, which already housed a monster treadmill that I had purchased the year before from the University of Florida football team.

When I reported to the Superstars eight weeks later, I had added 15 pounds of new muscle on my shoulders and arms. Even though I had been a world-class runner for many years, the strenuous exercise routine that I had just put myself through was my first real introduction to multisport, multifitness training. For me, the best part of it all was that I did it in the comfort of my own home, exercising when I wanted to, for as long as I wanted to. Thanks to these home exercise machines and the sound training program that I devised, which stressed strength, flexibility, power, and muscular endurance, I came in third place in the preliminaries of the Superstars and moved on to the finals. There I eventually finished behind such stars as James Lofton of the Detroit Lions football team and Renaldo Nehemiah, the world record hurdler and current player for the San Francisco 49ers football team.

Many people have asked me if the training program that I used for the Superstars could have helped me lower my mile or 5,000-meter running times if I had used it at the height of my running career. Unequivocally my answer is no. Distance running is a sport where bulk and extra weight are a hindrance, not a help. Yes, my home program did make me stronger and also quicker for running shorter distances. But for longer distance running, lean and light is always the best.

With the Superstars now behind me, a funny thing happened that I had never anticipated. I wasn't the one using the gym the most. My wife was. Carol has always felt that one runner putting in two daily workouts in the Liquori household was enough, so she never joined me in my running. Rearranging the family schedule for two runners, she said, would be impossible.

But lo and behold! A few months after I installed the exercise equipment in the house, I had to almost schedule appointments with Carol to get time to use the gym myself. With a new baby and no time to go to her weekly aerobics class, Carol found in the home gym a very good substitute for her missed classes. Once she put Michael down for his nap, she would put on her running shoes, turn on the treadmill, and go on a run. Boredom—one of the major drawbacks to aerobic exercise because of its repetitive nature (and something that can be magnified even more when you're exercising indoors)—was solved by watching the soaps on TV as she exercised.

Do you begin to see the possibilities that a home gym can open up for you?

Carol and I are different in our uses of the home gym. We had always had free weights in the house, but Carol never touched them. One day I commented on the obvious pain she seemed to be suffering

Exercising at home with Carol and Michael.

as she struggled along with a popular exercise video. I recommended that she try our multistation weight machine if she was so concerned with body shaping and toning. The machine was safer and easier to use than free weights, I explained, and I showed her some basic workouts. She finally took my advice a few weeks later, put away her videotape, and began a modified weight program to go along with her treadmill running and cycling. She was very pleased with the results.

Carol has made great strides since we installed the home gym. After just a year of indoor workouts she became hooked on jogging. She finally admitted that she had always felt self-conscious and foolish about running outside because the jocks and jockettes on the roads made her feel physically inadequate. Since she began her home workouts, however, she feels stronger than ever before. Those former inhibitions have vanished, replaced by a new confidence that I am very happy to see.

The home exercise market has exploded since I first jumped in, and stores are now virtually inundated with a lot of good, worthwhile pieces of home gym equipment. Unfortunately, there's a lot of bad equipment as well. Looking back now to my first foray into home exercise, I see how much the home exercise equipment market has grown and improved. After testing and putting many machines through their paces over the past six years, I eventually replaced all of my initial purchases with lighter, more compact, durable machines.

I consider myself a demanding athlete and I expect a lot from myself and from my equipment. There's nothing worse than getting all psyched up for a good workout, only to have to cut it short because of faulty exercise equipment. I'm always checking the market, trying out new pieces of home equipment as they come along. From my own experiences I have come to know what equipment is acceptable for home workouts and what just won't do.

The Heart of the Matter

Competitive running has always been an important part of my life. But now that I'm more your Average Joe than world-class runner, I find that exercising at home on different exercise machines offers me just as much emotional and physical release as my competitive running once did. My home aerobic workouts are sometimes as strenuous as my outdoor running workouts used to be. My legs get wobbly and my arms grow weak as I put myself through a varied routine that may include treadmill running, cycling, rowing, cross-country skiing, and weight work. I'm exhilarated by these workouts because they test the limits of my mind and body, and I look forward to them every day.

The old saying was that once the legs went, you were all washed up as an athlete. But it's really not the legs, or the abdomen, or the back, or the arms that matter the most. The most important muscle in your body is your heart. Exercise research has consistently pointed out that by exercising aerobically—moving vigorously and steadily within the boundaries of your target heart range for at least 20 to 45 minutes 3 times a week—you are doing all you can to strengthen the heart, improve over-all circulation, and raise the level of your fitness. The best way to exercise the heart and to keep the entire body fit is through running, skipping rope, swimming, rowing, cross-country skiing, and cycling. I've found that performing most of these activities on home exercise equipment that simulates them in a personal, concentrated, intense, convenient, efficient, no-nonsense manner is the best way to exercise. Home gym workouts eliminate the need to think of where, how, when, what, if, and what to wear. They strip away all excuses, leaving you only with the opportunity to have quality workouts 365 days a year.

The Health Club vs. the Home Gym

Exercising at home has been a gradual movement that for many started with a health-club membership. In the 1970s, large exercise-equipment companies such as Universal, Nautilus, and Cybex came up with exercise equipment that was "user friendly." Flashy, well-appointed health clubs sprang up around the country to bring this new dimension to a public that had gradually come to see muscle development and fitness as a safer and easier arrangement than the one offered by traditional black iron weights, ill-fitting exercise bikes, and hard-to-use rowing machines. Health clubs now prosper to the tune of $5 billion annually, in large part because the American public has come to see exercise machines as a key ingredient in their success in fitness.

Health clubs definitely serve a purpose. The good ones help beginners learn how to use the equipment properly, teach them how to exercise safely, and give advice about nutrition. In the better clubs, dedicated instructors and the over-all professional atmosphere lend encouragement to all.

Until recently, the health clubs had vastly superior equipment than what was available for the home market. But all of that has changed in the mid-1980s. Now, almost any piece of equipment that can be found in a health club is also available in a home-size version as well. And that's why I now work out exclusively at home.

Today, more and more people are justifying the cost and the space needed for a home gym. The concept of the 1990s is the dream house with a gourmet kitchen, hot tub, computer, video machine, and home gym. For many of us, these things don't seem so farfetched anymore.

A Gallup poll recently found that personal health is the number-one criterion on which people measure success. It's not surprising to find in 1984 that Americans bought 2.4 million exercise bikes, 3 million barbell sets, 450,000 rowing machines, and 727,000 multistation weight sets in an effort to achieve and maintain good health. It's estimated that by 1990 the home gym market in this country will be a $2.5 billion industry.

I swear by my home gym. Sometimes when I'm particularly tired or just don't feel like working out, I often swear at it. But all in all, I'm extremely happy to have the exercise equipment in the house. Glancing in the mirror after I finish a workout, I see the muscles and the added bulk. I'm often forced to wonder what happened to that skinny runner who ran 13:15 for 5,000 meters and had the best in the world chasing after him on the track. No, it's not that I feel fat now. Today I'm 6 feet, weigh 158 pounds, and am probably in better all-around condition than when I was at the height of my running career. Good all-around condition to me means speed, flexibility, strength, and general good health.

Sometimes, though, when the weather is great and I'm passing an outdoor running track with some spring in my step, I think about getting skinny again. There's no better feeling for me than to have no injuries, sunken cheeks, spikes, a rubberized running surface under my feet, and perspiration trickling down my skin. I get excited when I think about how it feels to take off the sweats on a cool night in Stockholm, Paris, or Oslo and have twenty thousand fans screaming at the top of their lungs, calling my name as I come off the last turn and sprint for the finish line.

Nah! Maybe when I'm forty and eligible for Master's running competitions. For now, I'm content with the new me and I'll take my workouts at home, thank you.

If I can have successful home workouts, so can you. All you have to do is get the equipment that you will be happy using, set a goal of at least three 30-minute workouts a week, and then surround yourself with

Learn how to make your home exercise routine fun and challenging. Invite a friend over.

the means to do it. Be consistent. Pace yourself by spreading your workouts evenly over the course of the week. But please, whatever you do, don't try to be a hero by going for record times, the highest speeds, or most weight lifted in your first workouts. You can possibly injure yourself doing this, or at least get sore muscles that will ache for a week. In such a physical state it's not uncommon to quickly abandon all thoughts of exercise forever.

The real secret to working out at home is moderation. Take it slow and easy, exercising at a comfortable pace that gets your heart beating at a steady, elevated rate. Little by little the results will start to come.

Where there's a will there's a way. This book will certainly give you many ways to exercise at home, and I hope that with the variety presented here, you will be able to find the will to begin and continue exercising today, tomorrow, and for the rest of your life.

THREE

THE TEN COMMANDMENTS OF HOME GYM WORKOUTS

WITH MORE THAN TWO DECADES OF EXERCISE BEHIND ME, I'VE come to understand the full meaning of fitness and its effect on both my physical and mental well-being. By regularly exercising in my home gym I am able to cope with the stresses of a busy workday and maintain my health (and sanity) at the same time.

Regular weekly exercise is important to me. I can't remember the last time I missed a workout, or, for that matter, the last time I was sick. In addition to exercising at home at least three times a week, I also run about 40 miles a week outdoors, play tennis, ride my motorcycle on dirt trails, and go boardsailing.

I firmly believe that exercise is critical to maintaining good health.

It's also fun to do. But knowing how to exercise properly to attain the maximum results is something that far too many people don't even understand. At the very least, not knowing basic exercise principles will cause you to have a less than satisfying workout. The attendant frustrations that come from a string of bad workouts can make you want to give up exercise altogether. All because you were never taught the basic tenets of exercise!

By following the ten exercise principles that I have laid out here, you will have at your fingertips the foundation of home exercise—all that you need to know about how to exercise safely and maintain your health. By supplying the necessary energy, you'll soon be on your way to a new, healthier you.

THE TEN EXERCISE PRINCIPLES

1.   SEE YOUR DOCTOR
2.   MAKE FITNESS A YEAR-ROUND ACTIVITY
3.   SET REALISTIC GOALS FOR YOURSELF
4.   MONITOR YOUR PULSE REGULARLY
5.   ACHIEVE THE TRAINING EFFECT
6.   DEVELOP MUSCLE BALANCE
7.   DON'T SKIP WARM-UPS AND COOL-DOWNS
8.   DON'T BE COMPULSIVE ABOUT YOUR EXERCISE PROGRAM
9.   ADD VARIETY TO YOUR WORKOUTS
10.   KEEP A TRAINING DIARY

---

1. See Your Doctor

If you are about to start a home exercise program, consider these questions before you begin.

1.   Do you smoke more than ten cigarettes daily?
2.   Are you overweight by more than 20 pounds?
3.   Are you thirty-five years old or older?
4.   Have you ever had a heart attack?
5.   Is there a history of heart disease in your family? Did either of your parents have a heart attack before the age of sixty?
6.   Have you ever had an abnormal stress electrocardiogram (ECG) test?

7. Have you ever thought that your heart was beating too fast?
8. Do you have arthritis?
9. Is your range of motion limited in any of your joints?
10. Do you have any chronic illnesses?

If you answer *yes* to one or more of these questions, you are a "medical problem" and shouldn't start exercising at home without proper clearance from your physician. Whatever you do, don't believe that you're not a medical problem. "But I played football in high school and ran a 2:50 marathon a few years ago," you might say. Yes, but that was a few years ago, and the Law of Reversibility has already set in. This law states that if you don't use your muscles regularly, then they will gradually start to lose their strength. This includes the strength of your heart and lungs as well. In extensive tests conducted by Dr. David L. Costill, director of the Human Performance Laboratory at Ball State University in Muncie, Indiana, it was found that even the most gifted distance runners are indistinguishable from the sedentary population after six to twelve months of inactivity.

So, before you start exercising and possibly seriously hurt yourself, be honest and admit to yourself that you first need a medical check-up. Without a complete medical exam you may bring on musculoskeletal problems or worse—a life-threatening heart attack.

Before beginning any exercise program, check with your physician first to see if you have any particular health risks—heart problem, arthritis, bad back—that could limit your participation in cycling, running, rowing, skiing, weight lifting, or whatever other home workout you choose. A cardiovascular exam and musculoskeletal exam to check joint stability is also advisable. It's also good to have a nutritional evaluation in order to see which foods should be eliminated or added to your present diet.

If you don't have a regular physician, you should find one. Also, if you feel that your present physician is best suited for treating illness rather than for educating you how to lead a healthier life through proper exercise, start your search for a new doctor. Ideally, he or she should have been an athlete or at least had experience working with athletes or sports teams. Doctors who regularly run, cycle, swim, ski, play tennis, or lift weights are generally good choices, because their exercise pursuits show that they pay more than lip service to the benefits of regular exercise.

According to Dr. L. Fiske Warren, a leading New York City–based orthopedic surgeon and team doctor for the New York Mets baseball team, people should ask friends for their recommendations of doctors.

Dr. Warren also recommends that you contact your local medical association or call the nearest medical school for their recommendations of certified sportsmedicine physicians.

A good national guide that lists sportsmedicine treatment centers is another way to find a new physician. This list can be purchased for $10 by sending a SASE to *The Physician and Sportsmedicine Magazine,* Attention Frances Caldwell, 4530 West 77th Street, Minneapolis, MN 55435. Ask for their Sportsmedicine Directory.

It may take time and effort, even weeks, before you eventually find the right doctor, but you owe it to yourself to spend the time. Apply the same intense scrutiny you might devote to looking for a good auto mechanic, a plumber, or a house painter. I certainly hope that your own health is worth more to you than getting a good brake job or a leaky faucet repaired. If it is, then treat it with even more seriousness. It's your physician who will be able to work along with you, giving you advice and monitoring your progress. If some condition does come up in the pre-exercise test that he administers, or if you subsequently injure yourself and can't continue to work out at your favorite home gym routine, your doctor can best help you by redirecting your interests, slightly modifying or completely changing your exercise program to suit your needs and capabilities.

2. Make Fitness a Year-Round Activity

Fitness can be achieved and maintained if your exercise is *rhythmic, continuous,* and *vigorous.* In order for your exercise to have any sustained benefit, you must exercise within the confines of your target or training heart zone for at least 20 minutes three times a week. Research has shown that some fitness gains can be made by exercising at this intensity twice a week. But to raise your fitness to a higher level, you have to increase both the intensity and the duration of your workouts. Working out only once a week has not been found to be productive at all.

Surely you can make space in your busy day to exercise. If you only gave 30 minutes, three times a week, this would be a mere 1½ hours out of the 168 hours in the week. Ride your exercise bike while watching the news on TV; go for a run on your treadmill before breakfast; get in a good rowing session after work; or lift weights to your favorite record before dinner. Exercise before meals has proved to be an excellent

Your home gym equipment is light and portable. Use it indoors or outdoors depending on the season.

appetite suppressant, because your body uses its own fat for fuel and releases a certain amount of it into your bloodstream. This automatically raises your blood-sugar level, which then diminishes your appetite.

Many times during the course of a week I'm very busy because of work or family obligations and I often find that I just can't make the time to go for a run through the woods on my favorite trail, or take a bike ride around the back roads. But, since installing my home gym, I don't worry about this anymore. I can slip on a pair of shorts and running shoes and step into my home gym. Now I'm ready for weights, rowing, cross-country skiing, bicycling, or running. There's no fuss, no bother. Forty-five minutes to an hour later I'm showered and dressed, ready for my next activity.

You should make regular home workouts part of your lifestyle. You'll not only feel good and look better, but regular exercise will also help:

- *Decrease your chance of having a heart attack or stroke by improving your circulation and metabolism.* Regular exercise lowers both your heart rate and your blood pressure and helps clear life-threatening plaque from arteries by changing your cholesterol profile.
- *Reduce the number of colds and flu attacks.* Some scientists believe that the proteins released when you exercise—endogenous pyrogen—are the same ones released when your body is combatting bacteria. In both cases, this protein raises your body temperature. A heated-up home exerciser, like a feverish nonexerciser, is therefore able to effectively fight germs and infection.
- *Alleviate depression by giving you a feeling of accomplishment and self-worth.* Some researchers feel that regular aerobic exercise can be as effective as psychotherapy in treating some forms of mild depression. In a study conducted by University of Kansas researchers Lisa McAnn and David S. Holmes, Ph.D., forty-three moderately to severely depressed women were assigned to one of three programs: aerobic exercise three times a week; no exercise; leisurely walks four times weekly. After a five- and then a ten-week check-up, it was found that only the women who exercised regularly and vigorously showed significant fitness gains and reduced depression levels.
- *Prevent osteoporosis, a painful and crippling bone disease.* Eight times more common in women than men, osteoporosis affects an estimated 20 million Americans. Scientists believe that regular exercise is a good way to prevent osteoporosis because it causes the muscles to pull on the bones, thereby stimulating them to absorb more calcium and other minerals from the body. This then thickens and strengthens the bones.
- *Bring about significant weight loss by burning large amounts of calories.* Cycling at 13 miles per hour will burn a whopping 300 calories in just 30 minutes. Walking, running, cross-country skiing, and rowing are also good aerobic as well as calorie-burning activities that will help you become slim and trim.

Contrary to what many distance runners, physicians, and exercise physiologists have previously thought, exercise alone—even if you run more than 100 miles a week—will not automatically grant you immunity from life-threatening factors such as stroke and heart attack. But it has been proved that once you improve your level of physical fitness, any unexpected physical strain will certainly be less demanding and therefore less life-threatening for you.

An exercise study conducted by researchers from the universities of North Carolina and Washington has pointed out that regular exercisers have a much lower risk of dying suddenly of a heart attack than do sedentary men. These scientists discovered that sedentary individuals who devote fewer than 20 minutes a week to vigorous exercise have a 56 times greater risk of dying of exertion during their normal activities than do those who exercise for more than 20 minutes daily. "Vigorous exercise," noted the researchers, "does seem to protect against sudden death from heart attack."

In yet another study, Dr. Ralph Paffenbarger, Jr., of Stanford University, found that of the 17,000 Harvard University male graduates between 1916 and 1950, those who exercised through midlife, burning at least 2,000 calories a week (this equals about 3.5 hours of jogging or 5 hours of brisk walking), were more likely to survive a heart attack than were their sedentary classmates. The active Harvard men, Dr. Paffenbarger discovered, had a 31 percent lower risk of dying from heart disease than did the moderately active Harvard alumni, and 46 percent less risk than the very inactive.

To be effective, home exercise should be done on a regular basis. Often, however, you may find yourself away from home or running late at work, so that you just can't exercise when you want to. Many people I know tell me that they start to feel guilty about missing their home workouts. What I tell them is that they should never feel guilty about missing an occasional workout or become overly compulsive about having to stick to a predetermined workout schedule. By developing a healthy attitude about your home exercise program—it's part of your life, not your entire life—your enthusiasm for exercising will always remain high.

Another common question I'm often asked is, "How do I motivate myself to exercise?" I realize that many people find it difficult to get themselves in the mood to move around and break into a sweat. There are days when I myself just don't feel like working out. There are many reasons for this, of course. Personal stress and not getting enough sleep are probably the most common ones. What I often do when I'm not feeling in top form is to look at my home exercise program as an elixir, a cure-all for that blah feeling. I know that if I exercise for only 20 minutes I will feel better later. On many occasions I have forced myself to exercise even though initially I didn't feel like it. But, after the first 5 minutes, the sweat starts to bead up on my forehead and I suddenly begin to feel renewed. I feel stronger, as if energized by some internal power I have unleashed. By the time I'm finished, I feel totally refreshed and happy that I didn't skip the workout.

3. Set Realistic Goals for Yourself

One of the chief disadvantages of working out at home is that you have to be your own coach, inspiration, and motivating force. This being the case, take the time to sit down, take out a pen and paper, and write out both *long-term* and *short-term* goals that you would like to achieve from your exercise program. Try to make your long-term aspirations exciting, challenging, and attainable; they should be reachable in at least one year to eighteen months. Some examples of long-term goals include:

- losing 50 pounds
- gaining 25 pounds
- increasing the size of your biceps
- decreasing your dress size
- gaining flexibility and being able to touch your toes
- decreasing your resting heart rate by 25 beats
- making the "tire" around your waistline disappear
- pedaling 6,000 miles in one year
- dropping a minute off your mile running time
- increasing your bench press by 100 pounds

Short-term goals are important as well and serve to bolster your spirits, motivate you, and encourage you to continue with your program. They should be attainable in one to twelve months. Some of these short-term goals include:

- losing 10 pounds of body weight in 6 weeks
- being able to walk/jog 2 miles without stopping
- lowering your resting pulse 5 beats
- gaining more stamina and zest in your life
- rowing nonstop for 30 minutes
- carrying two bags of groceries up two flights of stairs without getting winded
- adding 2 inches of muscle to your chest, arms, or legs
- cutting back or eliminating smoking and drinking

- losing 2 inches from your waistline or hips
- cycling 50 miles in a week

Goal setting is important if you are serious about continuing your home exercise program. Once you are able to admit to yourself, define, and then verbalize what it is that you really want from your fitness program, you will be better able to achieve your aims.

It's very important in goal setting that you don't neglect the cosmetic benefits of exercise. Psychological studies have revealed that most people exercise not so much because they're worried about their heart and over-all health, but because they're concerned with their body image and how they look.

You're probably the same way. Therefore, any program that you design for yourself should be part aerobic (cardiovascular in nature) to strengthen your heart and lungs. But, just as important, it has to be partly cosmetic in order to improve your appearance. If your exercise program doesn't help you achieve your cosmetic goals—shapely legs, taut stomach, smaller hips, bigger arms, subconsciously the things that you really want from your exercise program—I assure you that you'll quit your home program in no time.

Once you've had your physical exam and have written down your goals, put some reins on your enthusiasm and start your exercise program *gradually* and with caution. Fitness cannot be achieved overnight, but will come only through regular weekly workouts of at least 20 to 45 minutes. Just think how long it took you to lose what fitness you once had. Was it five months? A year? Four years? Be patient. Be diligent in your approach to exercise and I assure you that you will soon start to see some changes in both how you feel and how you look.

4. Monitor Your Pulse Regularly

You have a built-in computer in your chest that gives out all kinds of vital and accurate information twenty-four hours a day. Unlike any other machine, this one functions better and lasts longer the more it's used. This remarkable machine is called your heart.

Your heart is the strongest muscle in your body, beating an average of 100,000 times daily, pumping 4,300 gallons of blood throughout your system. The heart begins contracting at birth and stops at death, an average of 300 million contractions later. The heart has four chambers, two on the right side and two on the left. As you exercise, blood returns

Heart Rate Guide

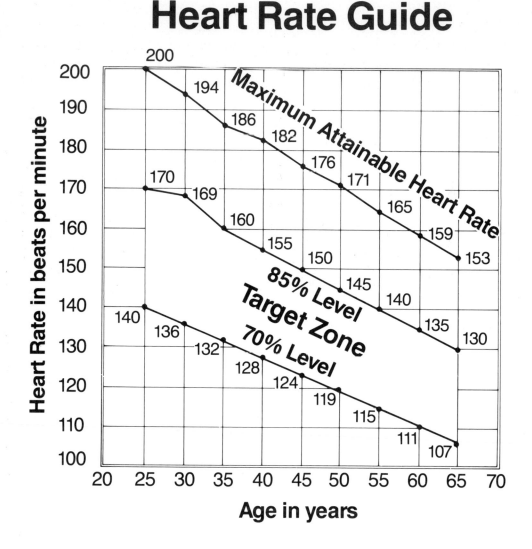

to the right atrium depleted of oxygen and carrying carbon dioxide from the working muscles. From there the blood is moved to the right ventricle, or pump, where it is pumped into the heart and the lungs to remove the carbon dioxide.

Oxygen-laden blood then collects in the left atrium of the heart and quickly moves to the left ventricle, where it is pumped out again to the working body muscles. The average resting heart will pump 40 milliliters of blood with each contraction. By contrast, the heart of a well-trained exerciser can pump as much as 100 milliliters.

Exercise will strengthen your heart and cause it to increase its size, just as it does any other muscle in your body. The fitter you become, the less the heart has to work, because of its increased strength and efficiency. Top athletes have resting heart rates in the 35–40 beats per minute (bpm) range, but they consume as much oxygen (0.4 liters per minute) as an untrained person does with a resting heart rate of 80 bpm.

The only way that the heart can reach its maximum efficiency is through regular aerobic exercise. By exercising aerobically (aerobically means "with oxygen") on a regular basis, working your heart muscle for a minimum of 20 uninterrupted minutes, 3 to 5 times a week, you will involve the large muscle groups of the body, thereby causing the heart to pump large quantities of blood to keep the muscles functioning at high levels of activity.

Rowing, running on a treadmill, and using an exercise bike or a cross-country ski simulator are excellent aerobic activities because they involve the large muscles of the body and will keep the heart rate sufficiently elevated. On the other hand, recreational activities such as tennis, bowling, golf, or weight lifting are generally poor heart and lung conditioners because they just can't keep the heart rate elevated long enough to achieve any significant benefit.

By regularly taking your pulse during the day and as you exercise, you will have sufficient information on which to base the following sound scientific decisions about your health and home exercise program:

- If you are too tired to undertake a hard workout and should modify the day's program or cancel the planned workout.
- Precisely when you are able to begin the stressful part of your exercise program.
- If you are working at sufficient intensity to ensure cardiovascular fitness.
- If you are exceeding safe limits to your heart and if you should cut back on your exercise level.
- When you can best slack off and then pick up your exercise pace for interval work.

Interval exercise, a training concept that was popularized in the 1950s, consists simply of making a series of repeated and intense efforts over a predetermined distance or for a predetermined time, with only a short rest period (or interval) between each effort. Physiologists have found that the greatest level of heart stimulation occurs during these brief exercise bouts because the heart is racing to pump the greatest volume of blood to the muscles. And, unlike the other form of training, called LSD (long steady distance), intervals, because of the short rest period built into the training, allow you to accomplish more intense exercise in shorter periods of time than does any other workout program available.

Your heart is the best indicator of how you are feeling and how much exercise you can safely tolerate. Your heart doesn't know distance or times or how fast you're going. Also, it doesn't matter to your heart if you are bicycling, running, rowing, or skiing. All the heart does is pump blood to meet the needs of your working muscles. If you're exercising strenuously, the heart beats furiously to keep up; slow down your workout and the heart slows down as well. And if you "red line" —push your body too hard for too long—your heart will let you know immediately by remaining at an elevated level, taking longer than normal to recover from that particular exercise bout. By simply taking your pulse you can find out exactly how your heart feels about your exercise program. With this information you can then safely design an exercise routine that will bring your heart and you the most benefit.

Taking your pulse and relying on your heart rate as an indicator of how you feel is the best way to safely and correctly monitor your exercise workout. By keeping your heart rate within certain parameters known as your target (or training) heart zone, you will be doing all you can to have a safe and successful aerobic workout.

If you are a newcomer to exercise, it's best that you monitor your heart rate several times during the course of each workout. After a few months of heart-rate monitoring you will reach a point when you no longer have to take your pulse as often. This is because you will have become so attuned to your heart that you will be able to correlate most exercise exertion with a pulse reading that falls within 5 beats, plus or minus, of your actual pulse.

Taking your pulse is a simple procedure for most people: using your three middle fingers, press lightly on either the radial or the carotid artery. The best place to take your pulse is on the radial artery located just at the base of your thumb on the left side of your wrist. Although the pulse can be also taken at the carotid artery, which is just below your ear and jawbone, just pressing there can sometimes lead to dizziness.

Count your pulse for 15 seconds and multiply this number by 4 to get your current resting pulse. The beats that you feel at your wrist and neck are the contractions of the heart as it pumps blood through the body. As you exercise, the heart beats faster to supply the muscles and tissues with more oxygen-enriched blood. As you taper off your workout, your heart beats slower until finally it levels off at your resting pulse rate.

To find your true resting pulse rate, take it *before* you get out of bed in the morning. Your morning resting pulse is the key factor in determining your current fitness level and state of health. An elevation of 5 to 10 beats over the reading from the previous morning is often an indication of possible stress, overwork, or oncoming illness.

Your age predetermines the maximum number of beats per minute that your heart theoretically is capable of. To determine your *maximum heart rate* (MHR), subtract your age from 220 if you are a man (this is the theoretical highest heart rate at birth; you lose 1 beat per year thereafter) or 226 if you are a woman. The number that you end up with is your current *maximum heart rate.*

In order to get the most from your exercise, you should exercise within a heart-rate boundary that is known as your *target heart zone.* This boundary is generally considered by exercise physiologists to be 60 percent on the low end and 85 percent on the high end of your maximum heart rate.

To achieve aerobic benefits from your exercise, you should first decide which percentage of your maximum heart rate you want to exercise at, and then try to keep it steady at that rate for at least 20 minutes of your workout.

To find your training heart rate, use the following formula:

Maximum Heart Rate − Resting Heart Rate × Desired percentage of Maximum Heart Rate + Current Resting Heart Rate = Training Heart Rate

Here's an example: I'm thirty-seven years old with a resting heart rate of 40 beats per minute. If I want to work out at 70 percent of my maximum heart rate on the low level and 85 percent on the upper level (I'm feeling ambitious this day), here's what I'd do:

1. 220 − 37 = 183 beats per minute, my age-adjusted Maximum Heart Rate.
2. Training Heart Rate = Maximum Heart Rate (183) − Resting Heart Rate (40 bpm) × percentage of Maximum Heart Rate (70 percent) + Resting Heart Rate (40 bpm).
3. Training Heart Rate = 140 bpm.

The same formula can be used to find the upper border of my training zone (85 percent) for the workout. The result is 161 bpm.

After a proper warm-up, these are the target rates that I should aim for and attempt to hold steady for at least 20 uninterrupted minutes of my exercise session.

Monitoring your pulse with your fingers is the least expensive way of taking your pulse but not always the best way. At times, though, taking your pulse by hand may be too disruptive to your workout. Dependable battery-operated heart-rate monitors are now on the market (see chapter 9), which use a small transmitter/monitor and a chest strap to take your pulse continuously while you exercise. Many models have built-in alarms that beep when you are below your target zone and buzz loudly when you are exceeding your maximum limit. To find your current pulse with an automatic monitor, you simply glance down at the monitor (which can be easily strapped to your belt, oar, wrist, or bike handlebars) and get an instant reading without interrupting your workout.

As you exercise and become more fit, your heart will become stronger and consequently not have to work as hard as it used to. This becomes evident in your resting heart rate. It will begin to decrease gradually as your fitness level increases.

5. Achieve the Training Effect

Exercising aerobically at least three times a week for 20 to 45 minutes per session will improve your cardiovascular fitness, tone your body, and help you to lose weight. But in order to make improvements in your home workouts—be able to lift more weight, row at a higher intensity, increase rpm's and resistance on the bike, ski at more tension, or reduce your mile time on the treadmill—you will have to gradually increase your workout intensity and duration. By systematically overloading your present workout level at a stress level greater than normal but no more than 10 percent of your previous level, working on specific muscle groups that are related to the task in which you are trying to improve, you will begin to see specific gains in your performance. This is called the training effect.

Proper stress and adequate rest are key elements in achieving the training effect. To become stronger and faster on your exercise bike, for example, you will have to start stressing your legs and cardiovascular system 10 percent above their regular exercise level and then allow them sufficient time to recover. I can't emphasize how important proper rest is for exercisers. Every time you have a particularly heavy exercise bout—you be the judge of what's heavy for you—your muscles develop microtears, actual slight rips of the tissue. It will take between 24 and 48 hours for them to heal completely before you can safely stress them once again. Then, too, when they heal they are slightly shorter in length than before, which is why you may feel stiff the day after a hard workout.

Before you begin your next workout be sure to have a proper warm-up period to stretch the muscles out to their normal length again. By using this stress and rest program—going hard one day, resting or going at it with much less intensity the next day—your muscles will grow and become stronger. This is the way that you move up to higher fitness levels.

How much stress you put on your muscles depends on you and your goals. All beginning exercisers will make huge fitness gains basically because they are so out of shape and therefore far removed from realizing their true athletic potential. Eventually, though, beginners will reach a plateau once the body accustoms itself to the stress (exercise) it's receiving. Some people are content to stay indefinitely at this fitness level, and they continue with their original running, cycling, rowing, skiing, or weight workouts at the same pace workout after workout after workout. There is nothing wrong with this, of course, but with no real physical challenge anymore from the workout, exercisers run the risk of boring themselves right out of home exercise.

Other home exercisers, after reaching a plateau and not seeing any more improvement, abandon their program altogether. Unfortunately, what they haven't realized is that for there to be any further improvement they have to raise the level of their work. This means increasing the exercise intensity, or exercising more frequently and for longer periods of time.

Those who want to see improvement in their workouts will have to start overloading their muscles on a regular basis, stressing them to a higher degree than before. Over a period of time, athletic improvement will actually be harder to achieve. This is because you are already exercising at your highest possible level. Gains will be only minimal at this high plateau, but don't be discouraged. Simply knowing that you are training at your fullest potential is a great achievement in and of itself and a major reason for personal satisfaction.

From personal experience, I've found that all aerobic exercisers, competitive distance runners especially, know the concept of plateaus. For example, young milers may run five 1-mile races in a row at times between 4:08 and 4:10. Then one day they may knock off a 4:05 for a personal best. After some quality rest, which could last for a week or longer, they start all over again with their training program, increasing the number of intervals, decreasing the rest period, adding on distance work, and finally leveling off at a 4:05 mile again. Then one day they push themselves a little harder and *boom!* a 4-minute mile.

For the home exerciser, like the young miler, the danger in training regularly without any break in training routine is that you will reach a plateau and then stay there too long. Yes, you may feel comfortable with your exercise program, but little by little your intensity will wane as you begin actually to stagnate physically and mentally. Both the body and the mind need a challenge from your exercise program!

There is a strong need in exercise to vary your workouts. Go hard one day, easy the next. Throw in a few 1-minute speed bursts during your workout to get your heart racing. Also, if you are ever going to break through these physiological and psychological plateaus, you have to include long rest periods to let your body recover and recharge itself. Every so often, after carefully building up the intensity and duration of your workouts, don't be afraid to test yourself with a "gut buster," a really hard workout that will push you to your max. Immediately follow this workout with a layoff of a week to 10 days. Yes, you can do light exercise in the meantime, but try to stay away from anything that will tax your body too much. Your body needs this time to rebuild, and you'll be much better off coming back to your home exercise program totally refreshed and ready to go once again, aiming for an even higher plateau than before.

6. Develop Muscle Balance

Exercise to strengthen both your agonist and your antagonist muscles during your workouts. Failure to do so could result in muscle pulls or structural misalignment. All of your body muscle groups come in pairs and must be strengthened equally. The agonist muscles are the prime movers of your body and they become short and inflexible the more they're exercised. The job of the opposing, antagonist muscles is to lengthen and restrict the range of motion of the agonists. But if these muscles aren't worked enough or specifically exercised, they soon become weak and prone to injury.

Here's an example: The biceps of your upper arms are agonist muscles; they allow you to bend your arms as you pull on your rower. They won't, however, allow you to straighten them out again. The quadriceps in the fronts of your thighs are also agonist muscles; they allow you to push down your pedals on your bike. They don't help you to pull up your legs.

As these agonist muscles become stronger through exercise, they also become thicker and shorter. Unless the respective antagonist muscles that oppose them—the triceps and hamstrings in this case—

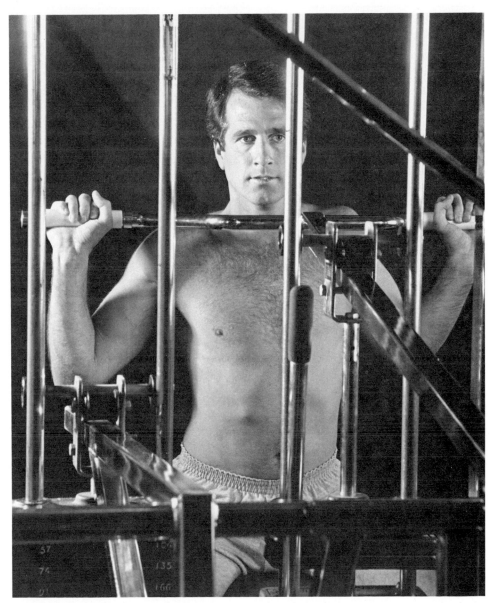

For proper muscle balance be sure to work all muscle groups equally.

are equally as strengthened, the antagonist muscles remain long, weak, and unable to do their job of controlling the speed and extension of the joints that the agonists are moving. It's this agonist/antagonist imbalance that very quickly leads to muscle strains, muscle pulls, and chronic joint conditions.

It's not uncommon to develop muscle imbalance after exercising exclusively on one piece of aerobic equipment. On a stationary bicycle, for example, the thousands of pedal rpm's you do while using only the muscles of the fronts of your legs will greatly develop the quadriceps on the fronts of the thighs, while neglecting the hamstrings on the backs of the thighs. This muscle imbalance can lead to knee, hip, or lower-back problems if it is not corrected with a running program that will strengthen the muscles in the backs of your legs and lower back; or with a weight-training program specifically aimed at your hamstrings.

By being aware of your muscles and trying to strengthen equally all parts of a muscle group, you will be doing all that you can to ensure maximum physical performance and a minimum number of injuries.

7. Don't Skip Warm-Ups and Cool-Downs

Each home workout should start with a warm-up program of no less than 5 to 10 minutes, which will prepare the body for the upcoming stress. Effective and easy warm-ups include slow jogging, running in place, rapid walking, using a rower with no resistance, pedaling an exercise bike with light resistance, and using a cross-country ski machine with no resistance. By warming up before you exercise you will gradually raise your body temperature, stretch your muscles and prepare them for exercise, accelerate your heart rate, increase blood flow to the muscles, and prepare all the body joints for exercise by lubricating the articular surfaces with a naturally produced lubricant called synovial fluid.

You know you're ready to start your workout session when you begin to perspire or when your heart rate has accelerated 20 to 30 beats above normal.

Cooling down properly after your workout is just as important as a good warm-up. Your aim is to slowly return your cardiovascular system to almost a preworkout condition. Coming to a complete stop after a vigorous workout is not recommended, because it will cause a quick drop in blood pressure, which can put enormous strain on the heart and also bring on a potential for oxygen shortage to the brain. In some cases, dizziness or fainting can result. However, when you cool down prior to the end of your workout—simply by slowing down the intensity of your exercise program during the 5 or 10 minutes before you actually stop—you will decrease the likelihood of risk.

Muscle stiffness is often the result of not cooling down adequately after exercise. When you work out, your muscles shorten and tear slightly from the stress load you put on them. Lactic acid, a natural waste product produced by the muscles during exercise, will also build up during the latter stages of exercise and often may cause the muscles to ache. Don't be alarmed. This is normal and a temporary condition that can be greatly alleviated by a cool-down period. If you have bicycled, skied, or run on the treadmill, end your workout gradually with a cooling-down period of at least 5 minutes. This way you will prevent "pooling" of the blood in the large arteries of the legs as well as help the blood in its journey back to the heart. Cool-downs are also effective in speeding up the removal of lactic acid from the muscles.

I think it takes more dedication to make sure you cool down properly than it does to actually exercise hard! Cooling down, even to many top athletes, seems an unnecessary ritual, and many foolishly skip doing it altogether. But the effects of not cooling down will show up in your next day's workout. You'll feel stiff, your muscles will ache, and you won't "flow" as you go through your program.

I often had a difficult time getting in a proper cool-down period after a big race. Mobbed by the press, I had to stand around answering questions about race tactics and my competitors. Usually I had to then hurry out of the arena to catch a bus or airplane for some other city and another race. Therefore, I generally missed my cool-down. Inevitably, my next day's workout was a total loss because I was too stiff to move.

8. Don't Be Compulsive about Your Exercise Program

All exercisers have to find the right balance between being cautious and being compulsive in their home workouts. Understanding at which level to begin and how much to push yourself is something that you have to learn by yourself if your program is to succeed. Many people, beginnners especially, make the mistake of working out at too high an intensity, thinking that the harder they strain and push on their machine, and the more pain they feel, the more beneficial the workout will be. This is a big mistake!

For home aerobic exercise such as cycling, running, cross-country skiing, or rowing to be beneficial, it should be *rhythmical, vigorous,* and *continuous*. Far too many people, however, concentrate too much on the vigorous aspect of exercise and actually push themselves too hard. This leads to the frustration of having a poor workout (they're not strong enough to continue such strenuous exercise at the fast pace that they've set for themselves); disillusionment with themselves as exercisers when they can't achieve their predetermined goals; and the feeling that exercise is just too much work to continue on a regular basis. But exercise isn't hard work if it's done correctly.

Many veteran exercisers (who should know better) are just as guilty of overstressing their bodies, too often crossing the fine line that sepa-

Listen to your body. Exercise safely and sensibly.

rates work from overwork. Giddy with visions of new personal bests for elapsed time, distance covered, or weight lifted, they pedal harder on their exercise bikes, row for longer periods of time on their rowers, and lift more weight on their multistation gyms than they should. "No pain, no gain" is their battle cry. In their blind quest for excellence and athletic nirvanah, they very often mistake their resulting pain and injury for fatigue or physical weakness. Instead of allowing themselves enough rest, they return day after day to their gyms and force themselves through workouts even though they may actually be suffering from a muscle pull, a sprain, or even a more damaging condition.

To compound their problem, these compulsive workout artists try to exercise through their ever-increasing pain. Unfortunately, what they're working toward isn't better health, but a sure visit to the doctor.

The quickest and safest way to monitor your exercise intensity and protect yourself from injury is to check your pulse during your workouts, remembering to keep within the bounds of your target heart zone, or, more specifically, to train only at your target heart rate. Exceeding these limits can push your heart rate to unsafe levels, while not reaching your limit will keep you from achieving any long-term benefits from exercise.

When you want to exercise a bit more strenuously than before, a good rule of thumb is to increase the time you spend exercising—the distance you run, pedal, or row, or the amount you lift—only by 10 percent over your previous level. Once you start to move away from your previous exercise base, this 10-percent progression will provide healthful and certainly adequate stress levels. Trying to progress at anything higher than this will bring you from a safe overload condition to a potentially dangerous overstress situation that your body isn't prepared for. Injury, which is then followed by rest and rehabilitation, is often the end result of trying to do too much exercise when your body isn't ready for it.

9. Add Variety to Your Workouts

By adding variety to your home workouts and challenging yourself to an array of physical tasks during your exercise week, your interest level will remain high and you'll eagerly look forward to each workout. By carefully alternating the use of different home machines, you will also avoid common overuse injuries; using only one type of machine, whether it is a bike, rower, or treadmill, can bring on chronic injury or fatigue to those joints and muscle groups used specifically in that exercise.

Give circuit training a try. This is a system of exercise using different machines during the same workout. Ten minutes on a rower, ten minutes on a bike, and ten minutes on the ski machine is a common example of an exercise circuit. Working out this way can safely develop a much greater number of muscles to the exclusion of none.

Another way to keep your motivation high as you exercise is to listen to fast-paced music. Often I'll run on my treadmill while listening to some jazz or a Bruce Springsteen cassette; this helps me to get a hard workout. Music seems to work wonders especially when I'm not particularly motivated to exercise. The beat and tempo of the music help me subconsciously to get my own movements in pace with it, and my workout automatically moves up to a higher level without too much perceived effort on my part.

At other times I may just watch a movie on the VCR or a favorite television show. Once I reach my predetermined heart rate, I just keep it at that level and watch the show as I continue the workout.

No matter how sensible and well planned your exercise program is, you may find that working out at home by yourself may never have the pizzazz that you get from a cross-country run on a beautiful fall day, three sets of well-played singles tennis, or a 10-mile time trial on your bike with the summer wind whipping through your hair. In these outdoor activities, your partner, a crowd of appreciative spectators, or just the great outdoors can inspire you to exercise levels you have never attained before.

Unfortunately, you don't have these wonderful external stimuli when you exercise at home. This is where I find training tools such as pulse meters, bike computers, calorie counters, and distance monitors to be a great incentive. The feedback you get as you exercise, learning exactly how well you are doing at any given time during the workout, encourages you to go on. And since you are provided with hard data from these sophisticated devices, it's very easy to then accurately chart your progress from workout to workout.

I have found that having a rich fantasy life is also a great training aid. To set the mood for quality home workout I often imagine that I'm going head to head with a top opponent, whether he be a runner, skier, oarsman, or cyclist. Whenever I feel myself starting to slack off my workout pace, I immediately pick it up again by imagining that I've got just a slight lead over my mystery man. By keeping my pace for just another minute, another mile, 50 more strokes, or whatever goal I set for myself, I can hold off my imaginary opponent and keep him from gaining on me. This mental game works wonders, and to date I'm still undefeated and the holder of world-championship titles in long-distance running, cross-country skiing, rowing, and cycling.

Unless you are a highly trained athlete or similarly motivated person, with no partner to exercise with or compete against at home, you may sometimes find your exercise routines uninteresting. Even boring. This is not uncommon. But if it happens more often than you would like, try inviting a friend over to exercise with you whenever possible. I find that working out with someone else, being able to compare notes and strategies, is a good way to get your competitive juices flowing on those slow days. You'll also be amazed at how quickly the workout seems to go.

As I mentioned before, I find the VCR and television perfect training aids and companions for working out at home. During a workout session, try to use commercial time to speed up the exercise pace a bit.

For instance, when I'm on my bike I often set a goal of pedaling for 30 minutes at 95 rpm's with a heart rate of 140 bpm—except when the commercials come on. These one-to-three-minute breaks from the show mean it's time for me to increase the pace for as long as the commercial lasts. On good days I'll jump to 125 rpm's and try to hold it at a heart rate of 165. But generally I settle in at 115 rpm's and a pulse of about 155. When the show comes back on I'm breathing hard and ready for a more relaxed pace and pulse. Working out this way gives diversity to your workout and adds a bit of a challenge to yourself.

10. Keep a Training Diary

Consistency is a key element in your exercise program if you are going to achieve your goals. A record-keeping system that charts such variables as daily weight, morning resting heart rate, workout heart rate, specific exercise routines, and personal thoughts about your daily workouts is a handy reference of your progress. As you move along, you may find that you want to experiment with different exercise routines. With a training diary you'll be able to accurately note the effects of the new program, referring to it whenever you need to study any developing patterns.

There are several ways of keeping a training diary. Many people simply buy one of the training diaries sold in most sporting-goods stores. Although these diaries are generally made expressly for runners or triathletes, you can easily modify them for your own use.

I have used a blank notebook to record my running workouts and have done so for twenty years. I now have twenty of these books and refer to them whenever I need to adjust my training. For ease of reference I have also started keeping a separate diary for my home gym workouts, keeping it on the desk in my gym, where I can write down all the information just after finishing my workout.

Patterns emerge in your workouts that may not be noticeable in daily or weekly reviews of your training log. But after a few months of note keeping you'll get a sense of what your body is actually capable of. For the more serious athletes, these training diaries can hold the key to why you aren't reaching your full athletic potential. For instance, in both 1969 and 1971 I was ranked number one in the world for the mile. However, in 1974, after some subpar years, I went back to my diaries to see exactly what workouts I had done when I was the world's fastest miler. I then compared these workouts to the ones done in 1970, 1972, and 1973, when I hadn't run as fast. My diaries showed that since the time I was graduated from Villanova in 1972 I hadn't run in as many races as in either 1969 or 1971. This was an important discovery and one I hadn't really thought too much about, but it was obviously a factor affecting both my racing sharpness and my conditioning. Also, my diaries revealed that I hadn't done as much speed work and interval work on the track as I had when I was in college.

Armed with this vital information, I adjusted my workouts. Eventually this note keeping and a few hours of research paid off. In 1975 I ran a 3:52:2 mile, the fastest in my career.

A Note about the Exercise Programs

It's critical to the success of any home gym workout program that you, the exerciser, learn to listen to your body. Listen to how you feel during and after a workout, physically as well as mentally, and understand what makes you feel that way.

The training programs outlined here for the different home machines are geared for the beginner, the intermediate, and the advanced exerciser. By listing these exercise programs I'm *not* saying that these are the only routines you should follow at home. These programs serve only as a plan of attack to cover 20 minutes to 1 hour or more of exercise. Look at these programs as blueprints, different proven approaches to making your workouts interesting and productive.

Don't ever get bullied by any preplanned exercise workouts. You shouldn't feel that you have to follow the programs to the exact letter every time you exercise. What's crucial to your success as a home exerciser is that you are able to learn and then understand your body's reaction to a particular workout. For some, this understanding may come in a few weeks. Most people, however, start to get a basic comprehension within a few months.

If you do want to exercise, but perhaps not as intensely as you first thought, simply follow an LSD workout like one of the many listed in the following chapters. If that's still too hard (or too easy), make up your own workout. By knowing your exercise goals and ambitions, and by understanding how you feel and why, planning your workouts will no longer be a problem. In the process you will have gained control over your own body.

Over time, with enough workouts written in your training diary, you'll become your own coach. Success with your home equipment means that you not only understand the mechanics of how each machine works, but, more important, that you can now get the best workout possible while using that machine. I hope that the exercise programs listed here will be a big help in that direction.

Know Yourself

The only way you will ever have a successful training program is to design one that will combine suitable amounts of LSD and interval work and still suit your particular needs and capabilities. Too often exercisers are influenced by how far, how fast, and how much their neighbor is working out. By trying to duplicate the exercise programs of their neighbors, they only doom themselves to failure, because they aren't addressing their own personal fitness needs.

A cardinal rule of exercise that I stress is never try to keep up with anything but your own training diary. Most of what you read or hear about someone's training is pure exaggeration. Some internationally ranked runners do this intentionally. One marathoner I know kept his training log in kilometers. So, instead of writing "6 miles" in his diary he would write "10 kilometers" for his day's workout. When he went abroad to race he would always leave the diary out on the bed for his roommate and fellow competitor to see. What the roommate would see penciled in would be weeks of 160–170, hoping to psych him out. In actuality this was 160–170 kilometers, a shockingly high number. or 90–100 miles, a typical workout for a distance runner.

Incorporate long steady distance (LSD) workouts and intervals into your own home program and mix them wisely. If you gear the workouts to your own capabilities, available time, and how you feel that particular day, you will achieve all that you possibly can from your exercise.

Long Steady Distance

Long steady distance (LSD) workouts are just what the name implies. When you have an LSD run, bike, row, or ski session in your home, you are exercising at a moderate pace for 20 minutes or more at 60 to 75 percent of your target heart rate. Once referred to in the running community as long slow distance workouts, the "slow" aspect has been dropped in the past few years and replaced with an emphasis on steady movement. Training at a steady, slightly elevated heart rate is much more beneficial to your heart and lungs.

The good thing about LSD workouts is that they are based on *your* current physical condition. Running on a treadmill or using a NordicTrack ski machine for 45 minutes at a 10-minute-mile pace may be LSD training for you. Stick with this program, use it as your aerobic foundation builder, and you will start to see changes in your strength, speed, endurance, and waistline.

For me, however, the 10-minute-mile pace is too slow to be beneficial. Why? Basically because I'm in better aerobic condition than the 10-minute miler and need to run at least a 6-minute mile in order to achieve any worthwhile aerobic benefit.

The key to a successful LSD workout is that the workout should fatigue but not exhaust you. The talk test is a good indicator of your workout intensity: if you're able to talk normally as you exercise, you are at the right level of exercise intensity. However, if you find yourself gasping for air as you exercise, slow down—you're pushing yourself too hard.

LSD workouts have many benefits:

1.   You develop your aerobic system through steady-state training. Your endurance also increases as you strengthen muscles used in the exercise. Over time, you're soon able to exercise longer and more efficiently.

2.   Exercising at a steady pace for 20 minutes or longer strengthens and expands capillaries to supply more oxygenated blood to working muscles.

3.   Your heart size increases with LSD training. This is a normal adaptive situation brought on by the heart's increased pumping to supply all

the working muscles with oxygenated blood. The trained heart is therefore stronger and better able to supply blood to the exerciser. Should you cut back on your exercise or stop it altogether, your heart and other body muscles will decrease in size and performance abilities.

4. Your resting heart rate will drop, but the athletically trained heart now has the capacity to pump blood more efficiently and powerfully than before.

5. Blood pressure will decrease.

6. LSD workouts are gentle, rhythmic, and not too taxing on the musculoskeletal system. People of all ages and exercise levels can benefit from them.

7. With the reduced stress level of LSD workouts you are able to learn proper form and work on perfecting it as you exercise over a longer period of time.

8. LSD workouts can be carried out day after day. Since you don't produce lactic acid in LSD workouts, you won't feel stiff or sore when you're finished. You can come back the next day renewed and eager to exercise once again.

9. LSD workouts put vitality back into your life. Your performance level on your home gym equipment will increase through LSD training. This helps increase your strength and endurance for performing all your regular day-to-day activities. You'll find that you now have more energy and tire less easily than before.

10. With a solid fitness and endurance base built from LSD training, you can safely move on to sprint and interval workouts with little or no problem.

Intervals

Interval workouts consist of a series of repeated sprints—look at them as exercise-intensity peaks—done over the same distance or for the same length of time, at approximately the same speed or cadence, with only a short, controlled rest period between each sprint.

Intervals are tough. They're tough to do and tough on the body, tearing down the muscles just as a hard weight workout does. What intervals actually do is force your heart rate up close to your maximum. This brings on a certain degree of physical fatigue, preferably as you are ending your interval. After each interval, you slow down your exercise and (1) either allow your heart rate to drop to a predetermined pulse rate or (2) take a rest for a predetermined period of time. Once you reach your lower pulse rate, or when your rest time is over, the sprint is started again.

In either case, using pulse or time to determine your rest period, you don't allow your system to fully recover from your exercise bout. The partial recovery made during rest periods allows your system to resynthesize lactic acid, while at the same time training your heart to pump more blood and pump it more efficiently before you start exercising at almost full speed again.

Why do intervals if they're so hard? For one thing, they're challenging. You are forced to push yourself almost to your limit and hold it there for a length of time. Being able to do this several times in a row is a personal accomplishment.

Research has also shown that intervals allow fit individuals to improve quickly by letting them accomplish a lot of work (exercise, training) in a relatively short period of time. While LSD workouts have you rolling along at 70 percent of your maximum heart rate for periods of 45 to 90 minutes, intervals have you repeatedly hammering away at 85 to 90 percent of your maximum heart rate for short bursts. Because of this intensity, fitness gains will be greater and come faster than with any other way of training.

INTERVAL DON'TS

1.   Don't begin interval training of any sort until you have built an adequate endurance base. LSD exercise will give you this necessary foundation. Moving from the slow, rhythmic pace up to the fast tempo of intervals takes very careful planning.

2.   Don't start interval work without a proper warm-up. You risk injury to muscle and joints if you begin your exercise without preparing the body for the impending stress. Warm-ups get you physically and mentally prepared for the rigors of intervals. Jumping right into intervals without a warm-up is too stressful and you'll probably quit before getting a beneficial workout.

3.   Don't *ever* do each interval at top speed. Hit your maximum output only near the end of each interval. Intervals are supposed to build power, speed, and strength and still leave you with enough energy to complete the next interval.

You want to work hard when you do intervals, but you don't want to push yourself to complete exhaustion. Gear your workout:rest ratio to 1:3 or higher (or lower) depending on your physical condition.

Example: Go hard on your home equipment for 30 seconds. Then go easy for 90 seconds before you go hard once again; or go hard for 1 minute, then easy or rest for 3 minutes.

Another way of doing intervals is to work off your pulse. Exercise to 150 bpm (higher or lower if you choose), hold it for 1 minute before stopping, then rest up until your pulse drops to 90 bpm. Once it reaches this, sprint out for another minute. Repeat several times.

In either case, once you become adept at performing intervals you won't need to be so dependent on clocks, watches, or pulse meters for delineating your work and rest periods. You will be able to tell when your body has recharged itself sufficiently during the rest interval to start work again.

4. From workout to workout, don't always exercise at the same distance, rpm, or intensity of effort when you do your intervals. Be willing to lower and raise your limits to give yourself some variety in the workouts. "Ladders" are great ways to bring this about. Here's a good example:

Perform your tasks (pedal, row, run, or ski) hard for 15 seconds, then slow for 45 seconds; go hard for 30 seconds, then slow for 45 seconds; go hard for 45 seconds, slow for 45 seconds; hard for 60 seconds, slow for 45 seconds. The aim in doing ladders is to progress in regularly spaced increments of work and rest. When you reach the top of the ladder—you set the limit—work your way back to the bottom once again in regular hard intensity/rest sequences.

5. Don't continue with your planned interval program if you feel overly fatigued or disinterested. You be the judge of your body and the coach for your workouts. If you have been doing intervals for several weeks, you will know how you should feel during the workout. Continuing to do intervals when you feel "burned out" will only lead to injury. When you don't feel good about going hard for the workout, just switch to an LSD workout. If that's too much, take the day off. Don't return to your exercise until you feel mentally and physically ready for the challenge.

6. Intervals are tiring and taxing to the body. Your muscles are overloaded and pushed almost to their limit by these difficult workouts. Because of this, you should allow for a 48-hour rest between interval workouts. You want to let the muscle tissue rebuild and keep yourself from burning out. Of your total week's training, intervals should compose only 10 to 20 percent.

PART II

HOME GYM EQUIPMENT & WORKOUTS

Equipment Overview

With our fast-paced lifestyle, exercising and working out at home has become the most efficient way to keep physically fit. Which exercise is the right one for you? Here at a glance are the benefits of the five major forms of exercise and the basic equipment needed to work out at home.

CYCLING

Equipment needed: Stationary bike or outdoor bike with wind load simulator.
Price: $80–$1,000
Benefits: An excellent aerobic exercise that almost everyone can do. Tones and strengthens the legs and buttocks.
How long: 20–45 minutes, three times weekly.
Calories expended per hour: 550
Precautions: Can cause knee and back problems if you use exclusively high-resistance settings or improperly adjust your saddle and handlebars.

WEIGHT TRAINING

Equipment needed: Free weights or a multistation weight unit.
Price: $100–$4,000
Benefits: Of all exercises, weight training is the best for strengthening, toning, and shaping every muscle in the body.
How long: 20–45 minutes, three times weekly.
Calories expended per hour: 450
Precautions: You must follow exact lifting techniques or risk straining muscles, ligaments, and tendons. For safety reasons, use a spotter when working with very heavy free weights.

ROWING

Equipment needed: Rowing machine.
Price: $300
Benefits: An excellent cardiovascular and body-toning exercise combined into one. Works the heart, lungs, legs, back, arms, and stomach.
How long: 20–45 minutes, three times weekly.
Calories expended per hour: 600
Precautions: Not recommended for people with lower-back problems. The initial tendency is for beginners to set the resistance setting too high, which generally results in a low-cadence, short-duration workout. Rowing is an arm and leg exercise that must be done with a certain degree of coordination in order to achieve maximum benefit.

WALKING

Equipment needed: Motorized or nonmotorized treadmill.
Price: $700–$3,000
Benefits: An excellent cardiovascular exercise that puts minimal stress on the joints. Great for toning and strengthening the legs, hips, and buttocks.
How long: 20–45 minutes or longer, three times weekly.
Calories expended per hour: 325
Precautions: Be sure to wear comfortable walking shoes.

RUNNING

Equipment needed: Motorized or nonmotorized treadmill.
Price: $700–$3,000
Benefits: An excellent cardiovascular conditioner. Tones and strengthens the entire lower body.
How long: 20–45 minutes, three times weekly.
Calories expended per hour: 635
Precautions: Good, comfortable running shoes are a must because three to five times your body weight comes crashing down on each footfall. This constant pounding can lead to muscle soreness and foot, knee, and lower-back problems.

CROSS-COUNTRY SKIING

Equipment needed: Cross-country ski machine.
Price: $500
Benefits: Every muscle group benefits from this aerobic exercise. A great exercise for people of all ages and physical abilities.
How long: 20–45 minutes, three times weekly.
Calories expended per hour: 650
Precautions: It takes some coordination to combine the poling action with the kicking of the legs. If this proves difficult, just hold on to the front pad.

HEART-RATE MONITORS

Equipment needed: Heart-rate monitor
Price: $160–$300
Benefits: Exercising according to your heart rate is the best way to work out. Quality heart-rate monitors are accurate to 1 beat and let you know your pulse instantly as you work out. No longer do you have to interrupt your workout to take your pulse by hand.
Precautions: Some people have faint heartbeats that some monitors are unable to detect. Be sure to try the monitor before purchasing it.

FOUR

STATIONARY BIKES

Why Cycle?

Bicycling indoors is a fast and gentle ride to fitness. Follow a regular cycling schedule of 20-to-45-minute segments three times a week, and you will strengthen your legs, the largest muscles in your body. Especially important is the added strength that cycling gives to the muscles, tendons, and ligaments surrounding the fragile knee joints. A cycling program will also slim your calves, tighten your buttocks, and tone your thighs.

Another major benefit from using a properly fitted exercise bicycle is that because you are sitting as you exercise and your upper body is supported by handlebars, little stress is put on your joints. Stationary cycling is therefore an excellent aerobic conditioner that's especially good for those people whose back or joint disorders prevent them from participating in other forms of exercise.

A regular cycling program also will bring about a reduced resting heart rate, strengthen lower-back muscles, expand the blood-transport system, and metabolize body fat at a very high rate.

What to Look for in a Stationary Bike

The level of enjoyment and the healthful benefits you will obtain from your cycling program depend mainly on the quality of bike that you purchase. A poorly designed and manufactured bike is not going to be enjoyable to use and is bound to end up in the attic, in the cellar, in a closet, or out at the curb for the garbageman. Buying a cheap bike won't save you money in the long run. After you find that your bargain bike doesn't work as well as you had hoped, you'll have to go out and spend more money on a quality bike that does work.

Components

Stationary bikes have come a long way from the clunky-looking models of ten years ago. Today's streamlined, slimmed-down versions are good-looking, lightweight, anatomically designed machines packaged with electronic gadgetry capable of measuring everything from time, distance, pedal rpm's, calories burned per minute, and total calories burned during each workout.

When deciding which bike to buy, read over the following key components of the exercise bike and know what you should be aware of *before* you make your purchase.

FLYWHEEL

The most important part of any bike is the flywheel, that heavy, solid wheel of steel located just below the handlebars. It's the weight of the flywheel and whether it is precision balanced that ultimately determines how smooth your ride will be. If the flywheel weighs less than 15 pounds, the bike will most certainly give a rough ride. The force that most people exert on the pedals, and therefore the flywheel, is enough to make a featherweight flywheel skip and clatter when you start to push the pedals at high rpm's/high resistance. This is a definite drawback, and I would advise you to stay away from these bikes. There is no one I know who has put aside the time to exercise who wants to contend with fighting a machine like this. Although many of these compact bikes look great (some even call them "sexy") and are easy to store, they'll never deliver a good workout.

You don't have to bring your own scale to the store to weigh the bike; just check the spec sheet. The Tunturi Professional Trainer has a 51-pound flywheel, the heaviest on the market, and the bike weighs 125 pounds. It's not surprising that this bike offers one of the smoothest rides available. But if you intend to buy this excellent bike and then move it around the house, you should think twice. The small wheels on the front of the Pro do make for easy transportation, but, as with any piece of home exercise equipment that may require taking it out of a closet every day or pushing it from room to room, it can become a tiresome chore. You may soon find that a heavy bike like this may become a major excuse *not* to exercise. If you really want this model, be sure to plan in advance where you will keep it, and if it needs to be moved, find out if you're strong enough to move it.

Precor, the home-fitness-equipment industry leader from Redmond, Washington, has deviated from the standard vertical flywheel and has come out with a radical new horizontal flywheel for its 830c Bicycle Ergometer. The precision-balanced flywheel on this bike weighs just 25 pounds and is housed under a covering at the base of the bike. Because of a unique West German direct-drive gearing system that turns the relatively light flywheel at three times the rotating speed of most stationary bike flywheels, the 830e gives a remarkably smooth and whisper-quiet ride. In addition to looking sporty, the 830e also has a very low center of gravity, making it the perfect bike for elderly cyclists who worry about their balance when getting on or off a bike. I'm sure that in the future most manufacturers will switch to the horizontal-flywheel design.

RESISTANCE REGULATORS

On bikes with vertical flywheels, the most reliable form of resistance comes from the strap system. To increase or decrease resistance on these bikes—making it harder or easier to pedal—you simply turn a knob located near the handlebar, and a nylon strap that encircles the flywheel gradually tightens or loosens its grip around the entire wheel. The tighter the strap on the wheel, the harder it is to pedal; the looser the strap, the easier it is to pedal.

The nylon-strap form of resistance is much more durable and reliable than the caliper brake system, the second type of resistance system available on exercise bikes. Calipers are generally found on all inexpensive bikes. Although both calipers and strap systems work by exerting pressure on the flywheel, as you change resistance on bikes with caliper pads, resistance is put on only one spot on the flywheel, making for an uncertain and at times jerky ride. A major exception to the caliper-brake generalization is the Tunturi Ergometer, a well-made caliper-braked bike that gives an excellent ride.

When you test ride a bike, notice how easy it is for you to reach the regulating knob that adjusts the tension. On some bikes the knob is located down near your feet and is difficult to reach. One thing you don't want to do during your workout is get off the bike, or have to bend way down near the wheel to adjust the tension. Do this too many times and you may not get back on the bike again.

To see how good a resistance regulator is, slowly turn the knob to change the tension as you pedal. You should feel a subtle, almost imperceptible change in the tension level. Your pedaling motion should remain smooth rather than uneven and jerky. What you ultimately want from your resistance regulator is fine tuning, the ability to make slight incremental jumps in tension whenever you wish. Bicycle workouts are tough enough without having the resistance jump from very easy to very difficult at the slightest twist of the knob simply because the bike has an unsophisticated tension regulator.

SADDLE

Do yourself a favor and get a good, comfortable saddle. You will be sitting on it throughout your workout, and if it's not comfortable, it's yet another excuse you'll have to skip your workout.

Serious cyclists who are used to the rock-hard, leather-covered plastic saddles found on most ten-speeds on the road today may be put off by the standard-issue saddles found on even the best exercise bikes. Newcomers to "one wheeling" generally opt for these broad, well-cushioned "fanny pillow" saddles. Of course, there's nothing wrong with these saddles. Remember, whatever feels most comfortable to you is what's best for you. In theory, however, a saddle is not supposed to cushion your bottom like an overstuffed armchair; it's designed to support the weight of your two lower pelvic bones. Although one would suspect that more cushioning would be better for you, actually the more cushioning a saddle has, the greater the tendency of your hips to roll from side to side as you pedal, absorbing the power that's put into each pedal stroke.

Of course, most stationary cyclists don't care about pedaling efficiency. They're just out for exercise rather than performance. Most of all, they want to feel comfortable as they put in their 20 to 45 minutes. If this sounds like you, then look for a well-cushioned seat when you buy your bike. One note of caution: the wider a saddle is—and almost all well-cushioned saddles are wide—the greater the tendency to restrict pedaling motion, chafe your thighs against the sides of the saddle, and cause you to bounce slightly on the saddle as you pedal. This could eventually lead to either a premature end to a promising workout or, worse, a dislike of stationary cycling.

I've heard many indoor cyclists complain that their bottoms hurt after using a particular saddle model. If you think you may have a potential problem with your bike saddle, look for a stationary bike that can be fitted with a variety of saddle models. Another option is to try a Spenco Saddle Pad. This ingenious elastomer polymer pad easily slips over your saddle in seconds, bringing relief to most people who have tried it.

Saddle Adjustment

"The ability to work on a bike depends on your comfort," says Ed Burke, technical adviser to the United States Cycling Federation (USCF). "Is your seat high enough? A good many times it's not the saddle that causes 'fanny fatigue,' but the fact that the saddle is set either too high or too low. You have to be very careful here if this is the case because an improperly adjusted seat stem can lead to serious knee conditions."

If your saddle is set too high, you'll hyperextend your knee. If the saddle is set too low, you could also damage your knees by overstressing the ligaments and tendons surrounding the knee joints. Tendonitis of the knee and chondromalacia, a softening of the underside of the kneecap, are not uncommon occurrences. Both hurt!

Here are some rules of thumb that can help you properly fit your bike saddle.

• Your saddle should be perpendicular to the ground. Some cycling experts find that men, because of their anatomy, may get a better ride with their seat tilted slightly upward, while women will be better off with a slight downward tilt to their saddle. If you're not satisfied with your saddle position, and your saddle can be tilted on your bike, try tilting it. I happen to be quite satisfied with the perpendicular positioning on my bike.

• When seated on your bike in your cycling shoes, place your heels on the pedals. You should be able to pedal backward with no

If you can pedal backwards comfortably with your heels on the pedals, then your seat is positioned at the correct height.

discernible rocking motion in your hips. Also, there should be a 15-degree bend in your knee in the downstroke position. Adjust your seat post accordingly.

HANDLEBARS

Drop handlebars are standard equipment nowadays on ten-speed bikes and on many stationary bikes as well. Although riding in the bent-over position may seem uncomfortable at first, especially for beginners, riding like this is actually the most efficient way. When you are bent over the handlebars, your lung capacity is increased, because your chest cavity is supported by your arms on the handlebars. You'll also get more

On many quality stationary bicycles the handles are adjustable. By simply turning a knob you can ride with them up or else down in the racing position.

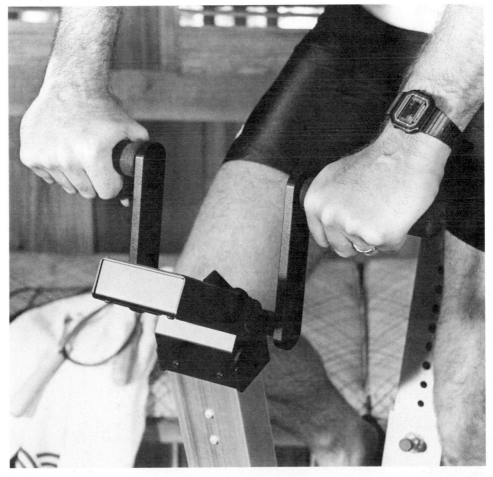

leg power, because you can pedal harder simply by pulling on the handlebars with your hands.

Handlebar height is a matter of personal preference and degree of fitness. Serious home cyclists often keep handlebars several inches lower than saddle height. Beginners should be more prudent. "Beginning stationary cyclists should keep the handlebars parallel with the saddle," says Phil Dunphy, a physical therapist and co-founder of the H.E.A.R. Institute (Health, Exercise, and Athletic Rehabilitation Institute), a state-of-the-art fitness and rehabilitation facility in Red Bank, New Jersey. "What do beginners care if they're going to get maximum use of their leg power by being bent over the handlebars. These people need to straighten their backs and sit in an erect position, a position most of them haven't been in all day. I recommend that they not even use the handlebars on the bike, but instead that they try to pedal with their backs straight and arms folded across their chest."

Some stationary bikes come with padded handlebars as standard equipment. If yours doesn't and you find that your hands are sore or numb after a workout, you can either wear padded cycling gloves or purchase handlebar pads at your local sporting-goods or bicycle store.

PEDALS

The most common pedal found on stationary bikes is the rubber platform pedal, an oversized flat surface that allows you to pedal in your socks if you wish. Unfortunately, many of the bikes with these pedals don't come with straps to hold your feet securely to the pedal. This becomes a problem once you start to pedal fast (85 to 100 rpm) and your feet constantly slip off.

I recommend that you get a bike that comes equipped with some form of foot strap on the pedal. If the bike doesn't have them, simply ask to have the pedals changed, an easy task on all quality bikes. Your pedaling cadence will increase dramatically when you use pedal straps, helping to make your workout more enjoyable and worthwhile.

Ergometers

If you want gadgets on your bike to measure your workload, how many calories you burned, how far you traveled, or how many pedal rpm's you're doing or how fast you're going, the price of your stationary bike may jump dramatically. What you will then be purchasing is an ergometer, a word derived from the Greek words for "measurement of work."

Don't discount the importance of an ergometer as a serious training tool just because of the increased price. The costly "bells and whistles" added on to a bike provide feedback that can make your workouts much more interesting and sustaining. Ergometers can also easily help you duplicate previous workouts as well as accurately chart your calories, rpm's, and distance. When used in conjunction with a reliable pulse meter, an ergometer can give you added incentive to continue with your exercise program.

For those of you with the money and space requirements, an excellent bike with its "bells and whistles" is the $3,400 Biocycle. This bike, from Engineering Dynamics Corporation, is completely computerized and comes with twelve programmed exercise levels. All you do is press a button and start pedaling. A graph on the screen shows you the prescribed course that you will have to pedal and exactly where you are on it. In addition to giving speed, rpm's, calories burned, and pulse, the bike also has an easy-to-read color TV screen that lets you race against a drone pedaling across the screen. When you finish your programmed ride, a fitness score based on how much work you did and how long it took you is displayed on the screen along with other pertinent information.

Wind Load Trainers

For those of you who already have a ten-speed bike, an alternative to purchasing a stationary bike is to buy a less costly, but equally effective, wind load trainer. These lightweight aluminum (15 to 30 pounds) stands have small twin fans on the rear that turn as you pedal; all work on the same basic principle of creating or simulating wind resistance. When you cycle outdoors, it is simply you against the resistance of the wind. It's estimated that only about 10 percent of your energy is used to actually propel the bike, while the other 90 percent is used to overcome the force of wind resistance.

On wind loaders, the faster you pedal, the faster the fans turn, sucking in air and then dispersing it, which makes it harder for you to pedal. Simply take off your bike's front wheel, mount the front fork of the bike to the front of the wind loader, and place the bike's rear wheel on the axle between the blower fans in back—then you're ready to ride. You can shift gears and pedal your bike on a trainer just as if you were

The shrouded fans and air tunnels on the Criterion wind trainer keeps a steady cool breeze blowing as you pedal away the miles.

outside riding down a straight road. The feel, strangely enough, is exactly the same.

Wind trainers were invented in the late 1970s and introduced at the New York bike show by Wilfried Baatz, a Seattle–based engineer who wanted to find a way to train on his $2,000 bike without worrying about daily weather changes. Baatz's original wind loader was called Racer-Mate and it became a big hit within the bicycle-racing community. But the word soon got out and Racer-Mate opened the floodgates for many imitations that are now on the market, most of which are actually quite good. Wind trainers now sell for $79 to $250.

When buying a wind load trainer, there are several factors to consider. The original Racer-Mate Pro Model is a top-mounted fan system. It puts constant pressure on the rear wheel and will not cause the wheel to slip as you jump up in speed or start to sprint. Bottom-mounted models will slip occasionally when you start to sprint.

Bottom-mounted or top-mounted, which is the best? For the competitive cyclist who wants constant, repetitive accuracy in his workout, the slippage from the bottom-mounted unit can be a drawback as well as an annoyance. So, for just about everyone but the true racer or the serious tourist, the bottom-mounted units are just fine.

Wind loaders are somewhat noisy. It's something like having a swarm of angry hornets trapped in a room with you as you pedal. Wind loaders also vibrate. A good recommendation for all apartment dwellers is to place a piece of plywood under the unit to cut down on floor vibrations, thereby keeping the downstairs neighbors happy.

Another precaution is to make sure that your tire is properly inflated to maximum pressure. If not, heat build-up and pressure will cause the rubber on the tread to flake off the tire.

The Road Machine is an excellent innovation on the wind-training theme. To use this solidly built unit, simply pop off your bike's back wheel, set your bike chain on the rear cluster of the Road Machine, tighten the rear fork, and you're ready to begin. This flywheel and fan system duplicates the rolling resistance felt by an 180-pound person riding a 25-pound bike outdoors at 32 mph on a straight road.

A major benefit of this home device is its compact size. And since you don't have to take off your front wheel, you're also able to turn the handlebars, thereby getting better balance on the bike. Getting out of the saddle and standing up on the pedals to crank away is not such a problem as it is on other wind trainers. The broad base of the Road Machine adequately supports even the heaviest rider.

How to Catch the Wind

Before you begin, make sure to do the following:

- Inflate your tire to the maximum pressure. An underinflated tire can easily lead to a mid-workout blowout.
- Prevent rusting of your bike and wind load trainer by keeping a towel draped over your handlebars. Be sure to dry off the sweat from all other uncovered parts of your bike with a towel after the workout to prevent corrosion. Dry off your wind load trainer as well to keep it from pitting and corroding.
- Fill up your water bottle before riding. You'll need to drink every 5 minutes or so in order to keep well hydrated. If it's very hot in the room, place a fan in front of you as you ride to cool you down, or else pedal in front of an open window.

How Much You Should Spend

As with all quality exercise equipment, choose a bike that fits your needs as well as your budget. A stationary bike in the $300–$400 range (current suggested retail price, discounts available nation-wide) will give you years of exercising enjoyment. Good bicycle ergometers, because of their sophisticated measuring equipment, will cost up to $800.

If this sticker price knocks you out of the exercise-bike market, there is one last recourse. If you have a ten-speed bike or can get a secondhand one, consider a wind load trainer as a practical and effective alternative to stationary cycling at home (see p. 59). Wind loaders range from $80 to $250.

Remember, you get what you pay for. There are certainly plenty of $100 bargain stationary bikes available at your local department or discount store. But take one ride on one of these bikes (if the salesperson will let you), and you'll see right away that the ride is uneven and unacceptable. The tension regulator is often difficult to reach, and once the tension is changed it won't stay at that level long before it starts to slip. If you do buy one of these products, your own tension level will surely start to rise, and in the end you will find out the hard way that bargain bikes are never really bargains after all.

"There are a lot of Taiwanese knock-offs on the market today," said Paul Byrne of Concept 90 Fitness Stores as we strolled down the aisle looking at all the home exercise equipment on display at the National Sporting Goods Association annual trade show in Dallas. "These Taiwanese stationary bikes are simply copies of designs and principles already long established by solid bike companies. They may look like good bikes but they're not; most of them are just plain awful. If you really want to see if a bike is good, just get on and try it. If the store owner won't let you do that, then you know there is something wrong with the bike that he's trying to hide from you."

Byrne recommends that when you go to look for a bike, you do the following:

* Check to see if it's easy to change the resistance as you pedal. Poor-quality bikes have dials connected to cables which then run to springs connected to a flimsy strap running around the flywheel. You can't make small increments in tension with these bikes and you have to continually interrupt your workout to adjust the tension. On a good bike, look for a cable running directly to the flywheel strap.
* Make sure you know in advance who is going to fix the bike if it should break. Good exercise bikes rarely break down, but when they do you don't want to be stranded without a workout while you hunt down a place to get it fixed. Your best bet is to buy your bike at

a full-service sporting-goods store that stands behind its products and guarantees repairs.

Form and Technique

You will get a more satisfying and beneficial workout from your stationary bike if you follow these simple bicycling rules.

CADENCE

Pedaling cadence is the continuous and rhythmic circular movement of your feet on the pedals. Learning to spin the pedals efficiently and smoothly between 75 and 90 rpm is the secret to successful, no-strain cycling. This high-rpm pedaling cadence is something to which every home cyclist should aspire. You will not only develop more leg speed and build up your heart rate and endurance by spinning the pedals, but your legs will become supple and loose.

The more you use your bike, the more you will see that your body seems to function best at a constant and comfortable cadence. Just as a comparison: Top road-racing cyclists spin the pedals in practice rides anywhere between 120 and 140 rpm; some even hit 200 rpm going downhill. Tour de France cyclists spin at 120 rpm throughout most of the three-and-a-half-week race.

Learning to spin the pedals fast in "circles" does not come naturally. Almost everyone's first inclination is to use a unilateral pumping motion: you push down hard with one leg, then push down hard with the other leg. The result is an inefficient, unnatural motion that will tire you quickly and make you want to get off the bike before you can reap any cycling or aerobic benefits.

Developing a good spinning technique will take hundreds of miles before it becomes second nature to you. But don't be discouraged. A close approximation of spinning will get you through your workouts just fine.

To pedal as efficiently as possible, try to visualize your feet turning in circles for the entire 360-degree pedal stroke. To carry this out, you have to concentrate on pulling up on the pedal, as opposed to having the leg pushed up by the force generated by the opposite downstroke. Straps, toe clips, and cleats will help you to accomplish this.

Spinning in circles is something that even the best racers in the world are working on constantly. The Italian cycling great, Francisco Moser, the current 1-hour distance record holder (31.7 miles) begins his preseason training by logging at least 1,000 miles on the road in low-gear, high-rpm workouts. This type of LSD workout not only builds his cardiovascular endurance but prepares his joints and muscles for the heavier workloads as his training period progresses.

This same training theory should be applied to your workouts. If you are just starting out on an exercise bike, *do not* use the high-resistance settings. You want to start out gradually (I can't emphasize this enough) at light resistance to introduce your body to the peculiar cycling stresses. Work on spinning the pedals with little resistance, and do your best to ride nonstop for the full workout time.

Your initial efforts at spinning the pedals may have you bouncing in the saddle, sometimes with the sensation that your thighs will hit you in your mouth. At times you may even feel like a hamster spinning on a wheel. But after a few workouts you'll become accustomed to the faster spinning motion. Initially, some leg fatigue will be felt when you finish your workouts. But this strain isn't so much from pushing against the resistance of the flywheel. It comes mainly from pushing the weight of your legs around and around the pedals.

With some conscientious practice you will develop the spinning technique and quickly notice that you'll be able not only to ride longer and faster but with much less fatigue than ever before.

Find Your Own Cadence

What you must do in the beginning stages of your cycling program is find a pedaling rhythm that is comfortable for you. Work out at that cadence whenever you exercise. Your goals when you use your stationary bike are as follows:

1. Pedal smoothly and consistently
2. Keep up a relatively high rpm, in the 70–90 range
3. Continue at a high rpm even as you increase the resistance on the flywheel

There is no single pedaling cadence that can be deemed "perfect" for all riders. The following is a quick way to find your natural cadence and the resistance level that is right for your workouts.

1. Select a resistance that lets you spin the pedals comfortably. Gradually start to increase the tension.
2. Once you have reached your training heart rate as defined by taking

Drink plenty of water as you ride to keep your muscles from overheating and cramping.

your pulse by hand or with a pulse meter, see if you are spinning in the 70–90 rpm range. You can find this by counting the number of times your right (or left) foot goes to the down position over a 1-minute period, or by simply referring to your bicycle computer (if you have one).

3. Adjust the resistance setting accordingly until you are spinning within the proper rpm range and are still at your training heart rate.

Over time your fitness level will improve. Your legs will become stronger and more accustomed to turning rapidly at this resistance. After a few weeks of training, when you begin to feel stronger, you can safely increase the resistance, once again maintaining the same pedaling cadence.

Stationary Cycling Tips

1. Don't let yourself become dehydrated during your workout. Drink water every 5 minutes, even if you don't feel thirsty. Lack of water as you ride will not only leave you feeling thirsty, but will cause your muscles to overheat and possibly begin to cramp.

2. Cycling indoors will get you sweating in a matter of minutes. If the exercise room is already hot, the combination of a sweating body and a hot room could make you feel as if you were in a sauna. Get a small fan and aim it up across your legs and upper body as you pedal. You'll welcome the refreshing breeze.

3.   Whenever you cycle, listen to your favorite music, turn on the TV, or watch a video. You'll be amazed at how fast the time passes.

4.   Make sure that your bike is properly maintained. Good bikes can go for months, even years, without maintenance. But even the best stationary bike will need some lubrication in order to keep giving a consistently smooth ride. Check your owner's manual for recommendations.

Bike Workouts

BEGINNER

Depending on your current physical conditioning, it can be rough going your first few days, sessions, or weeks on the stationary bike. It's not uncommon to feel a deep burning in your chest after a few minutes of pedaling. Your mouth will feel like it's filled with cotton and your legs will feel leaden. They may even cramp up and make you yelp with pain. If you do suffer cramps, get off the bike and knead the cramped muscle. Walk around a bit and get a drink of water. But then get back on the bike. Reset the resistance to a lower level and continue.

In your first session your aim is simply to become acquainted with your bike. On this first day out, if you feel good after 5 minutes of pedaling at a low resistance, try pushing the resistance up a little higher, pedal 40 to 50 turns, then drop back down to your original resistance. Do this several times until you get a feel for all the higher resistances and what they do to your legs and lungs. Remember, though, that this is only a test ride for you to see just what your bike is capable of doing.

In your ensuing workouts your goal is to *slowly* and *steadily* build an aerobic base for yourself. This means increasing the strength of your heart-lung package through steady-state or nonstop pedaling. This type of riding is also called LSD, an acronym for long steady distance.

Building an aerobic base is not accomplished by pedaling at a high resistance or by sprinting. That comes much later on in the program. "It takes weeks of steady LSD riding to build an adequate aerobic base," says Ed Burke of the United States Cycling Federation. "By pedaling at a steady pace that's below your maximum, you don't get overtired or, worse, burned out. You can come back to your next workout refreshed and ready to ride again."

According to John Howard, three-time Olympic cyclist, 1981 Ironman

Check that pulse! Here I'm using two Racer Mate wind loaders to provide maximum pedaling resistance.

Triathlon winner, and current world land-speed record holder on a bicycle (154 mph while riding behind a race car equipped with a wind faring, a large screen that shields the cyclist from the wind), any beginner who wants to seriously use a stationary bike as a conditioning tool should have a good pulse meter, pedals with straps or toe clips, and, if they have a hard saddle, a good pair of cycling shorts.

Howard recommends that beginners do the following:

- Choose an easy resistance setting on the bike.
- Keep track of pedal rpm's.
- Discover and establish your effective low and high training ranges.
- Work within this range, gradually increasing resistance, rpm, and time spent in the saddle. You know you're ready to move up when you finish a workout with little sweat on your clothing and feeling only slightly fatigued.

Over time, your short-term goal is to gradually raise your effective range while still keeping your pedaling rhythm. You can do this by simply pedaling nonstop for 30 to 45 minutes to build up your stamina. Another way to do it is through intervals.

Example: Current range is 60 rpm for 10 minutes of cycling.

Goal: In 1 month be able to pedal 80 rpm for 20 uninterrupted minutes.

Procedure: (Note that the letters M/W/F stand for Monday, Wednesday, Friday.)

M/W/F
Total time: 35 minutes
Target heart rate: 50–55 percent of maximum heart rate

10 minutes: Warm up, spinning in easy gear, low resistance to loosen and warm the muscles.

20 minutes: Workout consists of five 1-minute intervals at 75 percent of maximum effort. A good indicator of this effort is that you shouldn't be gasping for breath; you should be able to hold a conversation comfortably. Take a 3-minute break between each interval, spinning at a lower resistance.

5 minutes: Cool-down consists of pedaling at a lower resistance.

When you do the intervals, you have to try to maintain form and keep your effort as constant as possible. Don't surge or dip while doing them.

Once you can easily do this workout and can spin at 80 rpm for the allotted time, and also feel that you're too strong for the beginner level, move up to the intermediate workout.

INTERMEDIATE

Aim: To build endurance, strength, and power.

Begin LSD riding once again. This will help build another aerobic base for yourself. At least once a week you should pedal for 30 to 45 minutes (or longer if possible) at 75 percent of your capacity. You shouldn't be out of breath at any time during the workout. If you are, drop your resistance slightly or cut back on your cadence slightly. You're working too hard and defeating the purpose of a steady-state workout.

"Once a pedaling rhythm has been established," says John Howard, "the intermediate should once again mix his distance work [LSD] with speed work [intervals]. This adds balance to the program, building endurance as well as strength and power."

In the following workouts, remember to keep your pedaling speed elevated throughout the workout. The resistance is slightly higher than the beginner's level and the rpm's are increased.

WORKOUT 1

M/W/F
Total time: 35–55 minutes
Target heart rate: 60–80 percent of maximum heart rate

10–15 minutes: Warm up spinning in a low gear or low resistance.
15–30 minutes: Workout consists of 5 to 10 1-minute intervals using a resistance or gear setting that will let you spin at 90 to 100 rpm. Drop resistance after each interval, take a 2-minute break by spinning lightly, then start up again.
5–10 minutes: Cool down with easy spinning.

Other workouts to add diversity to your cycling week include:

WORKOUT 2

Total time: 30–40 minutes
Target heart rate: 60–80 percent of maximum heart rate

5–10 minutes: Warm up.
20 minutes: Cycle for 1 or 2 minutes at high resistance, keeping your form and cadence steady. Take a 2-to-4-minute rest break with easy spinning and then start up again. Try 4 to 6 reps.
5–10 minutes: Cool down with easy spinning.

WORKOUT 3

Total time: 22–40 minutes
Target heart rate: 75–85 percent of maximum heart rate

"Jumps" are a challenge to do and very tiring, especially as you approach the last ones.
5–10 minutes: Warm up.
12–20 minutes: Set the tension level almost to the maximum. From a dead stop, come up off the saddle and start cranking until you reach speed. Once you hit stride, sit back down and keep up the speed for 15 seconds. Reduce tension and spin for 1-to-2 minutes before starting up again. Do 5 to 8 jumps per workout.
5–10 minutes: Cool down. Don't do jumps 2 days in a row. They're very taxing on the body.

Coming out of the saddle and cranking away on a "jump."

ADVANCED

Workouts at this level are for the purpose of building higher levels of endurance, strength, and power, once again using a mix of LSD and interval training. These workouts are geared for the serious stationary cyclist and are used by top American road racers, modified and slightly scaled down here. Again, the emphasis is on establishing a smooth, steady rhythm. This will give you the aerobic base for future strength and power development.

WORKOUT 1

M/W/F
Total time: approximately 55 minutes
Target heart rate: based on individual exertion

15 minutes: Warm up in low gears to get your circulation going.
20 minutes: Using a heart monitor, find your maximum heart rate by *gradually increased* effort for 15 to 20 minutes of pedaling. When the heart rate *stops* increasing, stop your ride.
5–10 minutes: Cool down with very easy spinning.
6–12 minutes: Do four 1-minute intervals at about 20 percent less than maximum target heart rate. Allow the heart rate to return to a comfortable level before starting the next interval. Try to alternate between a medium-hard and a harder resistance on a stationary bike, or between a big gear and a small gear on a wind load simulator.
5–10 minutes: Cool down in low resistance.

WORKOUT 2

Total time: 45–60 minutes once or twice a week
Target heart rate: 75–85 percent of maximum heart rate

15 minutes: Warm up at low resistance to loosen the muscles.
15–20 minutes: Workout consists of steady-state time-trialing with the most resistance you can pedal. Make sure not to pass your level of training where you begin to get out of breath and surpass your target heart rate. Maintain 90–110 rpm cadence.
5 minutes: Light spinning to cool down.
6–14 minutes: The second part of the workout consists of intervals done just below maximum speed. Sprint for 15 seconds, then spin for the next minute before starting the next sprint. Do 5 to 10 reps.
5–10 minutes: Cool down with light spinning.

WORKOUT 3

Total time: 30–45 minutes approximately, once a week
Target heart rate: 70–85 percent of maximum heart rate

5–10 minutes: Warm up with light spinning.
20–25 minutes: Workout consists of jump training. Set your tension at the highest resistance. From a dead stop, come up from the saddle and pedal to the maximum, then sit down and hold this cadence for 15 seconds. Repeat up to 10 times during the workout, taking a 90-second break between sprints.
5–10 minutes: Cool down at light resistance.

WORKOUT 4

Total time: 60–90 minutes; can be done daily
Target heart rate: 70 percent of maximum heart rate

5–10 minutes: Warm up in low gear.
45 minutes or longer: With a comfortable resistance, pedal at steady state maintaining cadence throughout.
5–10 minutes: Cool down with light spinning.

WORKOUT 5

Total time: 35–45 minutes approximately. Never do two days in a row.
Target heart rate: 70–85 percent of maximum heart rate

5–10 minutes: Warm up at low resistance.
15 minutes: Set bike at high resistance. Do ten 30-second intervals with a 1-minute recovery period or less between each interval. Lower the resistance if you can't maintain your cadence, or if you start to feel weak.
10 minutes: Spin in slightly lower resistance at 90 rpm.
5–10 minutes: Cool down at light resistance.

Medical Problems

Strain and overuse are the most common causes of injuries that result from a cycling-only program. Following are the five most common medical problems and what you can do to treat them yourself.

1. *Sore shoulder and neck.* Sore muscles of the shoulder and neck are more common to beginners than to advanced stationary cyclists. This condition stems from holding on to the handlebars and supporting your upper body weight with your arms, which results in an eventual straining of the shoulder muscles and neck. The sensation is more discomfort than pain and can be alleviated by sitting up straight in the saddle as you pedal. If you choose to continue to hold on to the handlebars during ensuing workouts, try raising the handlebars a little bit. When the handlebars are set too low, your arms and shoulders bear too much of your upper-body weight, which brings on the strain.

2. *Saddle sores.* Saddle sores often come when you ride your bike for long periods of time. The sores are caused by friction between the saddle and your bottom and appear as small boils on the buttocks.

The best way to treat this problem is to wash the inflamed area with alcohol wipes; wear clean, dry shorts every time you cycle; and apply cornstarch or baby powder to your shorts prior to exercise to absorb all

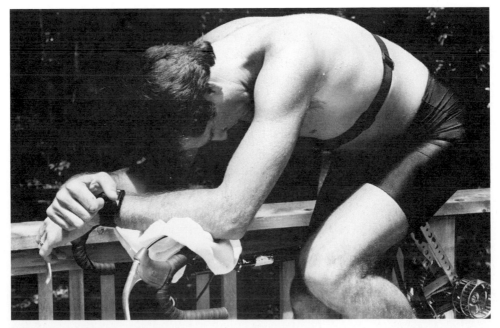

It feels good when it's all over.

moisture. Petroleum jelly applied to the buttocks before a workout will also help reduce the friction.

3.   *Leg cramps.* A cramp in your leg will feel like a sharp, searing pain and cause you to stop pedaling immediately. If you're lucky, the pain will be only momentary. Sometimes, though, it's so severe that you will have to get off the bike. Cramps can be caused by many different things: not enough salt in your diet, a potassium deficiency, or a fatigued or strained leg muscle.

Treatment for cramps is basic: Stretch the injured muscle by pulling up on your toes with one hand while kneading the muscle with your other hand. To prevent future cramps, increase your intake of potassium-rich fruits such as cantaloupe and bananas, drink more fruit juices, and drink plenty of water as you cycle.

4.   *Numb fingers and crotch.* Numbness to the penis or clitoris is often caused by compressing the pudendal nerves between the saddle and the pelvis. It is enough to scare you the first time it happens but is really no cause for alarm. The condition will clear up after a few days of not cycling. A good solution to this problem is to slightly raise or lower the angle of your saddle. If that doesn't work, try a new saddle design. There are many on the market.

Numbness of the fingers is another stationary-cycling ailment. The problem is generally caused by too much pressure being exerted on the heel of the hand as you hold on to the top of the handlebars. To date, rest is the only known cure. To alleviate the problem permanently, wear cycling gloves padded with Sorbothane, an excellent shock absorber. If this doesn't work, pad your handlebars with thick foam grips available in any good bike shop.

5.   *Tendonitis of the knee.* Due to the special biomechanics involved in cycling, this is perhaps the most common *major* medical complaint. Symptoms include pain in and around the kneecap, swelling, and a grinding noise as you pedal. Don't ignore tendonitis and think that it will go away by itself. It won't. Tendonitis of the knee is an inflammation of the tendons surrounding the joint. Pain is generally intense when you first wake up, but, strangely enough, it dissipates as you begin to walk around. Your knee(s) may not even hurt when you exercise on your bike. But the next morning . . . yikes!

Causes of tendonitis:

• Using too high a tension level on the bike for extended periods of time, or using a level of tension that doesn't fit your present conditioning level.

- Starting out in too high a tension level without a proper warm-up. Gentle warm-ups are recommended because they get the synovial fluid in your knee joints warm. This in turn will lubricate the knee and prepare it for the upcoming exercise load.
- Using a bike that's not properly set up will also bring on tendonitis. Having the handlebars, pedals, and saddle properly adjusted to your height is critical in achieving pain-free pedaling. In severe cases, treatment for tendonitis includes a minimum of two weeks' rest. The knee should be iced for three days, twice daily for 30 minutes. If you are able to address the cause of the problem, not just the symptoms, you'll be able to eliminate recurrence. Unfortunately, if not treated properly, tendonitis can lead to a chronic condition.

Select Equipment

The following companies manufacture quality home exercise bikes, ergometers, or wind load simulators.

Amerec Corporation
1776 136th Place NE
Bellevue, WA 98009
(800) 426–0858

Amerec doesn't manufacture its own equipment, but rather imports and distributes the quality Tunturi line of exercise equipment from Finland.

Tunturi Home Cycle Model ATHC

Length: 37.5"
Width: 20"
Height: 25.5"
Flywheel: 27 lbs.
Total weight: 53 lbs.
Cost: $280

This is Tunturi's basic home unit. Compact in size, it is a solidly built machine for the beginning or casual cyclist. Flywheel resistance is easily set by a fingertip switch on the handlebars. Comes with a built-in timer and odometer/speedometer.

Tunturi Home Cycle Model ATHC

Tunturi Racing Ergometer

Length: 37.5″
Width: 20″
Height: 42.5″
Flywheel: 40 lbs.
Total weight: 73 lbs.
Cost: $425

This is a bike for the serious cyclist. A European-styled racing seat and drop handlebars are standard equipment on this beauty. Precision controls to monitor pedal rpm, distance, speed, and resistance to the flywheel are featured accessories.

Cybex

Lumex, Inc.
2100 Smithtown Ave.
Ronkonkoma, NY 11779
(516) 585-9000

Fitron Cycle Ergometer

Length: 42″
Width: 24″
Height: 54″
Weight: 135 lbs.
Cost: $1,095

This price is no misprint. If you want to buy the Rolls-Royce of serious exercise bikes, this is the one to get. Manufactured by Cybex, the most respected name in rehabilitation equipment in America, the Fitron is a medically approved ergometer that uses a unique accommodating resistance system. Just dial in your desired pedal rpm rate, from 30 to 150 rpm, and start pedaling. The Fitron is isokinetic. This means that if you increase your speed, the bike will automatically increase resistance on your leg muscles over the entire range of pedaling motion; if you begin to tire, the bike will decrease resistance on the pedals. Seat adjustments are available to comfortably fit a 4′10″ cyclist as well as one 6′10″. This bike is required equipment in training rooms of most pro teams and a solid choice for anyone who can afford it.

Tunturi Racing Ergometer

Fitron Cycle Ergometer

Engineering Dynamics Corporation
120 Stedman St.
Lowell, MA 01851
(617) 458-1456

Biocycle

Length: 52″
Width: 26″
Height: 48.5″
Weight: 180 lbs.
Cost: $3,395

Videos have finally come to home exercise! Here's the home exercise bike for the person who has everything. You simply plug in this bike, start pedaling, and the handlebar screen lights up with all types of computer readouts. Workouts are measured in watts and calories. Pulse is taken when you hold on to the handlebars. The Biocycle comes with ten built-in training programs plus two that you can create for yourself, all controlled by a microprocessor. Select the program that you want, and as you exercise, the computer sets resistance as you move along. The unit is fairly large, but the wheels on the front make it relatively easy to move around.

Biocycle

Hooker Performance
1024 West Brooks St.
Ontario, CA 91761
(800) 854-9811

Criterion

Length: 43″
Width: 23″
Height: 20″
Weight: 40 lbs.
Cost: $250

Here is an easy-to-assemble wind load simulator/ergometer invented by two die-hard Ironman triathletes who also happen to be executives at Hooker Performance, one of the leading automotive-parts companies in the country. Looking for a way to

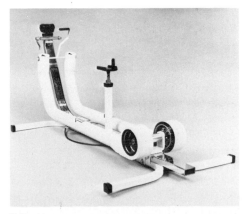

Criterion

train on their bikes when the California weather turned bad, they came up with the Criterion, a precision-crafted ergometer that will give you repeatable workouts of the highest caliber. The full system comes with a bike stand and air tunnels that run from the shrouded fans on the back all the way up to the front fork of your bike. As you pedal, air is sucked into the tubes and forced out and up toward your chest, keeping you cool and dry as you work out. An easy-to-read odometer/speedometer sits on the front of the unit, and an accompanying clip-on chart helps keep track of your work rate, pedal cadence, and total work completed.

Houdaille Industries
PO Box 3132
Fort Worth, TX 76113
(800) 772-6502

The Road Machine II

Length: 20"
Width: 26.5"
Height: 17.5"
Flywheel: 15.5 lbs
Total weight: 27.5 lbs.
Cost: $180

Houdaille has taken the wind load simulator another step by introducing the Road Machine II. This ultraquiet, very stable unit gives the best simulation of actual outdoor cycling conditions available on the market today. Since there is no bike tire rubbing on an axle as in other wind simulators, the Road Machine saves on tire wear and eliminates any problems of tire slippage. Assembly takes three minutes. To use the Road Machine, simply pop off your rear wheel, adjust your bike chain to the sprockets on the Road Machine, tighten two nuts, and start to pedal. Having the front wheel on makes a big difference in over-all stability.

The Road Machine II

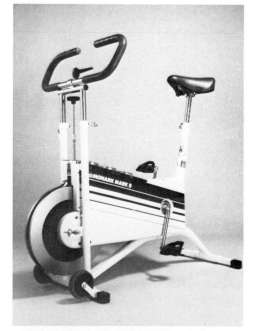

Mark II Ergometer 865 (p. 79)

Monark

Universal Fitness Products
20 Terminal Drive South
Plainview, NY 11803
(800) 645-7554

Mark II Ergometer 865

Length: 38″
Width: 21″
Height: 42″
Flywheel: 40 lbs.
Total weight: 75 lbs.
Cost: $575

This is a solid choice from the wide Monark line of bikes and is perfect for people who need an ergometer for heart-monitoring purposes. It comes with easy-to-adjust handlebars, a timer, and a speedometer/odometer.

Monark 875 Home Cycle

Length: 37.8″
Width: 21″
Height: 44″
Flywheel: 28 lbs.
Total weight: 64 lbs.
Cost: $325

The newest bike in the Monark line features adjustable handlebars, belt-strap resistance, and a speedometer/odometer. A solid bike for the money.

Monark 875 Home Cycle

J. Øglænd, Inc.

40 Radio Circle
Mt. Kisco, NY 10549
(914) 666-2272

Bodyguard 955 Exerciser

Length: 33″
Width: 16″
Height: 41″
Flywheel: 27 lbs.
Total weight: 60 lbs.
Cost: $340

Bodyguard 955 Exerciser

Perhaps the best buy for the money, the Bodyguard 955 Exerciser comes with a sturdy gear box mechanism that is the best in the industry. It also has rotating handlebars and an instrument panel that will note pedal rpm, speed, distance, and time. One drawback is the placement of the resistance regulator on the bottom of the bike, which makes it hard to reach as you pedal. Newer models come equipped with an extender.

Precor USA
PO Box 1018
Redmond, WA 98073
(800) 662-0606

Precor 820e Electronic Bicycle

Length: 25.5"
Width: 16"
Height: 42"
Flywheel: 25 lbs.
Total weight: 55 lbs.
Cost: $495

Precor 820e Electronic Bicycle

This is a rock-steady, quiet unit from the company at the cutting edge of home exercise equipment. Microprocessor-controlled electronics display elapsed time, distance, and pedal rpm. Sleek, high-tech profile and easy-to-roll front wheel make this unit a top choice for any room of the house.

Precor 830e Bicycle Ergometer

Length: 25.5"
Width: 16"
Height: 42"
Flywheel: 25 lbs.
Total weight: 60 lbs.
Cost: $800

The quietest ride of any ergometer, the 830e has a unique horizontal flywheel, and a highly accurate built-in microprocessor that displays elapsed time, pedal rpm, work rate in calories, and total calories ex-

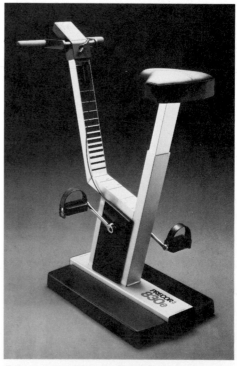
Precor 830e Bicycle Ergometer

pended. Padded handlebars adjust through a full 360-degree range. A superior bike.

Racer-Mate
3016 NE Blakely
Seattle, WA 98105
(800) 522-3610

Racer-Mate Original Pro Model

Length: 41"
Width: 17"
Height: 18"
Weight: 17 lbs.
Cost: $165

This handy aluminum wind loader connects to your bike seat post and sits on your wheel as you pedal, duplicating fairly accurately the road conditions of resistance and pedaling difficulty. The stationary stand holds your bike in place without the front wheel on, while another support in the middle of the stand holds the bottom bracket and keeps the rear wheel slightly off the ground. A fine training device for the outdoor touring cyclist or racing enthusiast.

Racer-Mate Original Pro Model

Racer-Mate III

Length: 41"
Width: 17"
Height: 18"
Weight: 17 lbs.
Cost: $130

This bottom-loading wind trainer uses the same double-bladed turbo fans as the Pro Model, but on this model the rear bicycle wheel is placed on top of the fans' axle. Set-up time is minutes, and with the new bottom-bracket support with universal centering device, the Racer-Mate III eliminates side-to-side movement of the bike that is so common (and annoying) with other trainers at high speeds.

Racer-Mate III

FIVE

WEIGHT TRAINING

Why Exercise with Weights?

Weight training is a popular way to develop endurance, strength, flexibility, and body tone. Weight training is also a good way to rehabilitate yourself after an injury or illness. Whether by pulling your body on a slanted board, pushing or pulling weights on a weight machine, or hoisting weights stacked on the ends of barbells or dumbbells, weight training can work every muscle in your body, making you fitter and stronger. However, unless done quickly in a circuit where you move quickly around in an organized pattern working one muscle group at each station, never resting more than 20 seconds between exercises, weight training will not be an aerobic activity and therefore will offer only little cardiovascular benefit.

Weight-training programs are generally the same for men as for women. Although most women lack significant strength in the trunk, shoulders, and arms, they can make huge gains in strength if they follow a carefully monitored, well-balanced weight-training program. Because of the hormonal differences between men and women (women lack significant levels of testosterone, the naturally produced tissue-building hormone), women will not develop the oversized muscles that men can develop from lifting weights. Instead, a firm, well-contoured figure is usually found among women who weight train.

"Men are generally attracted to free weights and big multistation weight machines to build strength and muscle mass," says Patricia Ripley, a New York City–based fitness consultant who trains both men and women. "I've found that women, for the most part, tend to be turned off by most home weight machines, instead going for either dumbbell exercise or else the Total Gym and the Precor 720 Inclined Exerciser. These two workout routines are certainly less masculine and less complicated than using a multistation machine, and that's what women are looking for in a strength or toning workout."

Phil Dunphy of the H.E.A.R. Institute (Health, Exercise, and Athletic Rehabilitation) in Red Bank, New Jersey, agrees. "Women aren't as mechanical-minded as men; they're intimidated by weight machines. And besides, most machines are physically just too big for many women."

Another problem, says Dunphy, is that the weight progression on the machine is generally in ten-pound increments, which is too high for most women to use safely. "A woman's upper-body strength is already twenty to thirty percent lower than an average male's," Dunphy explains. "Asking them to jump from ten pounds, the lowest setting on most machines, to the next setting, which is twenty pounds, is a hundred percent increase in weight. This is way too much for a woman. A machine that starts at ten pounds and then goes to twelve to fifteen pounds is a much more logical and safe progression for a beginner."

Unfortunately, most manufacturers didn't think of the female user when they designed their machines. The fact of the matter is that women will always have a difficult time on the weight machines simply because the machines are too big and the weight progression is too steep. Two alternatives to a home weight machine that women will have no trouble with are the Total Gym and the Precor 720 Inclined Exerciser. Both units are basically the same. They are manufactured by the same parent company. However, the Precor 720 Inclined Exerciser is a much more refined piece of equipment. Both will increase body tone, strength, and flexibility by using the exerciser's own body weight, which is pulled up and down on a sliding inclined board. "It's the 'poor man's Nautilus,'" says *The Runner* magazine senior writer, Hal Higdon, who works out on his Total Gym several times a week. "You can work your joints in a full range of motion on one of these machines," he says. "It can't be beat."

Establish Goals

Before you begin any weight-training program you should ask yourself what it is you want to achieve. Do you want to increase your strength? If you ride your bike 20 miles at a clip with no problem, but struggle to carry two bags of groceries back from the supermarket, then strength training is what you need. Working out with the heaviest weights you can manage for 4 to 8 repetitions (reps) of each exercise, with 3 to 5 minutes' rest between sets, will develop muscular strength. Because the muscles need to recuperate, don't work the same muscles two days in a row or more than three times a week.

Instead of gaining strength, do you want to tone your less-than-taut arms, stomach, buttocks, or thighs? If your skin droops over in folds and you think you look too much like the Michelin Tire man, then toning is what you're after. Weight workouts can give it to you when you perform 3 sets of 20 reps with heavy weights during your workouts.

Perhaps what you want most to achieve is muscular endurance, the ability to sustain an average effort over a long period of time. For you, muscular endurance could be the ability to put in a full day's work and still have the stamina to go for a round of golf, a few sets of tennis, or a jog in the park after work. Weight training can give you muscular endurance when you work with weights that are below your maximum lifting ability, progressively working up to 40 repetitions of each exercise.

Overload

No matter if your weight-training goals are toning, endurance, or strength, no matter if you choose to use a weight machine, free weights, or both, one training principle that is common to all is overload. This theory states that the human body can adapt to any increase in stress by simply becoming stronger and bigger. Every time you lift a weight, thereby effectively overloading the body with more weight than the body is accustomed to, you create an overload situation that the body will soon adapt to.

To overload your muscles safely you have to continually work them against a resistance greater than the one you normally encounter in day-to-day activities. This resistance is progressively increased once your muscles start to get accustomed to the weight load, creating once again a new overload situation.

Overload can also be achieved by increasing the number of repetitions and sets and the speed at which the weight-training exercise is performed. The choice is yours.

Until a sufficient strength base is reached, I strongly urge beginners to show restraint and restrict themselves. Keep the workouts light and easy so that the joints, muscles, and tendons can fully adapt to these new stresses. Otherwise you may be inviting serious injury.

Of all the home gym workouts, it is weight training that requires the most patience. For some people, perhaps someone like yourself, safely adapting to lifting heavier weights can take months of gradually increasing the amounts. Although you may feel like you're not progressing and want to give up and quit—don't. Results will slowly start to show if you keep following the basic lifting routines.

Body Balance

Unfortunately, many people confuse weight training with body building, thinking they'll start to look like body-building-great-turned-actor Arnold Schwarzenegger once they start lifting weights. What these people fail to realize is that there is a tremendous difference in approach, outlook, goals, and the amount of time spent with weights between themselves and a world-class body builder such as Arnold Schwarzenegger. In this chapter I will describe routines of weight training with machines or free weights specifically designed for improving over-all muscular balance, endurance, strength, or body tone. If all you want are big muscles like Arnold's, you won't find out how to do it here. Read one of Arnold's books on the topic.

Balanced body development is important in any weight program. By working the agonist muscles (muscles that start your movement by contracting) and the antagonists (muscles that lengthen and oppose the movement), you will condition each part of your body evenly. This will prevent a potential overload situation of a muscle group that could then lead to a serious injury to the arms, legs, midsection, back, or shoulders.

Weight Machines and Free Weights

There are two ways to weight train at home. The first method is with free weights, either dumbbells or barbells. Free weights got their name because they're not fixed to any machine, but are free to move as you move them through your body's range of motion. Free weights are the preferred choice of most highly trained athletes because little-used synergist or supporter muscles are called upon to assist your larger muscles in balancing and stabilizing the weights as you first lift, position, balance, and then move the weights through a particular weight-lifting pattern. By incorporating and strengthening these auxiliary muscles in a free-weight-training program, you can then develop a more explosive power that is unmatched by training only with weight machines.

The second way to train at home is with a weight machine, generally a heavy metal contraption that is a complete workout center all in one. These units consist of either a weight stack that is hoisted by pulleys and cables; a movement arm that is pushed against the resistance provided by heavy rubber bands; or a sliding board that uses the exerciser's own body weight to provide resistance at different inclines.

Both free weights and weight machines have advantages and disadvantages. What both do equally well, however, is overload the muscles, working them through a full range of motion, thereby providing flexibility, strength, endurance, and toning.

Weight Machines

Advantages

1. *Safety.* Weight machines offer the safest way to exercise with weights. In a home situation where you, or your children, may be working out alone, the safety of a machine is very desirable. On quality machines the heavy weight stacks are held by pulleys and cables and locked into a track. If you can no longer lift the load, or for some reason you have to let go, you can do so without fear of having the weights come crashing down on you.

2. *Muscle isolation.* Some machines are better able than free weights to isolate muscle groups that you may want to work on.

3. *Efficiency.* Weight machines offer efficiency of time and space. Since you can perform as many as 70 different weight routines on some

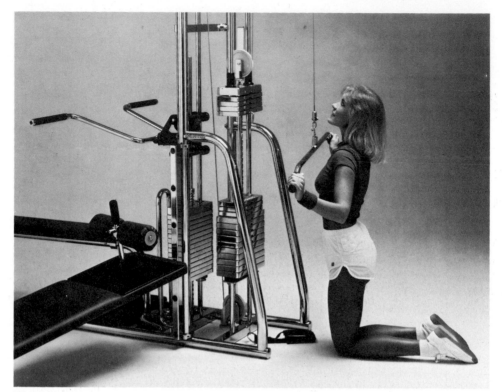

Weight machines offer the safest way to exercise with weights. Here's the Universal Power-Pak 400 with high pulley station.

quality multistation machines just by moving a cable or pulling a pin, your time is spent exercising rather than taking off and putting back on weight plates.

4. *Proper form.* Machines enforce proper lifting patterns. As you push or pull the weights, the machine guides you along a certain predetermined, fixed track, making it impossible to develop an improper lifting form.

Disadvantages

1.   Good machines are expensive. Quality machines start at $400 and deluxe machines can run $5,000 or more.

2.   The machines lock you into a particular movement pattern. This is a disadvantage for the more serious athletes because the machine will develop only the large muscle groups, ignoring the smaller synergist, or supporter muscles, which aid greatly in developing over-all power and strength.

3.   You can "cheat" on a machine by quickly pulling, pushing, or jerking hard on the movement arm. This force will move the weight stack and keep it going on its own momentum without putting full pressure on your muscles as it's supposed to do.

Free Weights

Advantages

1.   A free-weight program will develop the smaller auxiliary or "assister" muscles of the body that come into play as you balance the barbell or dumbbells in performing an exercise.

2.   A complete weight set and bench can cost $250—far less than a basic weight machine.

3.   Weights require little space and can easily be stored when not in use.

Disadvantages

1.   Training with free weights can be dangerous if you don't have someone to spot for you when lifting heavy weights. If you strain yourself or work yourself to fatigue, the weights can fall on top of you, causing serious and sometimes even fatal injury.

2.   If not secured properly, weights can easily become unbalanced, leading to injury.

3.   A large portion of a weight workout is spent changing the weight plates rather than working out with them. This is a loss of valuable training time for someone on a tight time schedule.

What to Look For in a Weight Machine

Components

If you have decided that ordinary iron free weights are not what you want for your home workout, go to your sporting-goods store or fitness center dressed in your workout gear to look for a multistation weight unit. You're dealing with a costly item, so don't be afraid or bashful about getting on the machine and using it. You're permitted to take a brand-new car out for a test drive, aren't you? Similarly, test drive your weight machine before you buy it. Ask the salesperson any questions you have about the machine.

There are several critical items to be aware of when selecting your home weight machine.

CHANGING POSITIONS

Ease of changing from one exercise to another on a weight machine is the most important factor in selecting a machine. A friend of mine found this out the hard way when he bought a weight machine that was on sale at a department store for $300. Sure, my pal admitted, using this particular machine would entail a lot of pulley and cable switching to go from one exercise to the next. Also, he would have to put the machine together himself. But the price couldn't be beat; it was $200 off the regular price. The savings would make up for the cable switching he would have to do. Or so he thought.

I did my best to discourage him from buying the machine. Three years earlier I had made a similar mistake when I bought a poorly made weight machine whose only redeeming quality was its low price. Unfortunately, my friend's mind was already made up to buy this shining chrome-and-steel machine and I couldn't dissuade him.

Shortly after he got it home he started dropping weight routines from his workout because it was so frustrating and difficult to unhook the pulley and cables to switch from one exercise to another. After a few weeks the initial glow of his exercise ardor died down and he began to skip workouts altogether because he didn't look forward to fighting his poorly designed machine. Three months after he so proudly set up his weight machine in his basement, his weight lifting came to an end. Not only out the money he spent on the machine, he also wasn't able to do the weight work that he had wanted to do in the first place. His weight-machine bargain turned out to be one of the worst investments he ever made.

Remember: A manufacturer may cram forty different exercise positions onto a home weight machine. But if you have to be a Houdini or a well-accomplished contortionist to do the exercises, you'll only stick to the easiest settings. After a while you'll be like my friend. Once the initial zeal starts to wane, the machine will only be used for hanging plants.

A quality weight machine will be first and foremost easy to use. Unclip a large cable attachment, hook it to the weight deck, and start lifting. That's all there should be to it. Look for nylon-coated aircraft cables on your machine. The larger the gauge, the higher quality the cable is. Pulleys should be heavy duty, preferably made of bronze. They should be able to swivel from side to side so that you can do different exercises from different angles without banging the cables into the tubing of the frame or the bench.

CONSTRUCTION

When buying a machine, check to see that the main frame of the unit is made of thick chrome-plated tubing that is welded securely together. If you have to use screws and bolts to hold the main frame together, it will eventually start to rattle and clank. It will never be sturdy enough to hold up to repeated workouts.

SIZING

When you are sitting on the weight machine, make sure that it fits you. This seems almost silly to mention, but the fact is that most of these machines accommodate only the manufacturer's preconceived notion of an average-sized person. In many cases the manufacturer didn't have you in mind. So, try out the bench, the leg extension/curl unit, and the "pec" deck, and see if it's comfortable.

If you have a long trunk, or long arms, short arms, or long legs, you may find that you're not the right size for many weight machines. Don't be foolish and think you can adapt to the machine. You don't adapt to shoes that are too big or a bicycle that's too small, do you? The same goes for weight machines. Working out on a machine that doesn't fit you properly can lead to some serious biomechanical problems that could eventually require medical attention.

BENCH AND ATTACHMENTS

On better machines, the bench is removable, enabling you to get more room for different exercises. Also, an independent weight stack for leg work allows more than one person to use the machine at the same time and also cuts down on your set-up time.

MACHINE MOVEMENT

Pull down on the handlebars. Does the movement feel smooth as the weight stack moves up and down? Or is it jerky, tight, uneven? A quality unit will have four sets of rollers and thick cables to ensure that the weight-stack tracks are friction free through the range of motion.

Check to see if there are heavy-duty steel springs on the bottom of each weight deck. Although you shouldn't let go of the weights and let them drop down to the bottom of the track with a crash, there will eventually come the day when this happens. If your machine is equipped with steel springs, it will cushion the weight fall considerably, protecting your machine and your nerves.

WEIGHT COMPOSITION

Look at the weights. Are they vinyl covered? If so, you can be sure that at some point the vinyl will crack from the constant pounding it receives in the course of each workout. Once this happens, the concrete "weight" inside will start to crumble right before your eyes.

What you want to see in your weight stack are iron or the more costly (you're paying for looks only here) chrome plates. Don't buy a machine with concrete weight plates. Iron can be hoisted, dropped repeatedly, and pounded together. Nothing will happen to iron plates. Of course, iron may be a bit noisier than vinyl-covered concrete weights, but it will give you years of trouble-free service.

The steel pins used for changing the weights should be accessible and easy to use.

While you're looking at the weight stack, be sure to find out if you can add more weight to the stack if the need arises. Some machines start with a basic load of 125 pounds and can take no more weight. Some others come with a higher basic stack weight and can take an additional 100 pounds at extra cost. *Remember:* Don't invest in a weight machine that you will outgrow in a few months as you increase in strength and power.

PADDING

Is the bench seat padded well enough and securely attached to the board? Naugahyde covering is preferred to vinyl and should be tightly stitched to prevent bunching and crimping. Make sure all your accessory pieces are well padded, especially the leg extension/leg curl unit. If there's not enough foam padding under the Naugahyde, you'll be in some pain and discomfort when working with heavy weights because the machine will press sharply into your shins or Achilles' tendons.

PURCHASE

When you finally find a machine that you like and want to buy, but can't afford, check to see if the manufacturer offers credit financing on the unit. Many companies offer this service to qualified purchasers. Once the paperwork is taken care of, find out who is going to deliver the machine to your house, who is going to set it up for you (or mount it on the wall for you if that's where you want it), and who will show you how to use it safely.

As with all quality home exercise equipment, by purchasing the unit from a reputable full-service specialty fitness store you can generally be assured of set-up, instruction, maintenance, and repair. Buy a machine from a pro as opposed to a department store, and let the pro take care of everything for you.

How Much You Should Spend

Once again, sticker shock may set in when you go to price a quality home weight machine. Expect to pay anywhere between $300 and $4,000, depending on how much weight you want and how many additional features you would like on the machine. Of course, you can get by spending only $300 for a machine and be quite happy with the quality and workmanship. If you're lucky, it will also fit your exercise needs. However, these low-priced machines are generally limited by their basic weight stack of 125 pounds and the inability to accommodate certain weight routines on the machine.

If you are just beginning a home weight-training program, you may want to make only a small investment in a machine. In the long run, though, it's important that you know what your capabilities are or will be. If you think you will outgrow your small, less expensive machine in a short time, don't buy it. Save your money for a larger machine rather than taking the smaller one and having to upgrade at a later date.

Iron Plates, Bars, and Dumbbells

Free weights—the weighted iron plates put on dumbbells or stacked on barbells—do just what their name implies: they have a free and unlimited range of motion that you, the exerciser, can control. And because you have to balance the weights and control and coordinate yourself to use them with the proper technique, most strength coaches agree that you can get a more complete workout with them than with a standard multistation weight machine.

Free weights give you unlimited range of motion.

What to Look For

If you decide to purchase free weights, determine first who will use them and where they will be used. If the weights are for you or your children and will be used in a garage, cellar, or somewhere else where you're not concerned about damage to a floor or carpet, buy the cheapest iron weights you can find.

However, don't skimp when it comes to buying your iron barbell. Make sure it's at least an inch thick, weighs 15 pounds or more, and comes with iron collars to hold the weights in place. Weight clips are quicker and easier to use than collars, but if you happen to be holding the bar and then tip it with the weights, clips generally aren't strong enough to hold the weights in place. Iron will surely come crashing down onto the floor—or your feet!

If you intend to take your free weights out of the dark cellar and into sunlit rooms and you are interested in good looks and quality in weights, chrome-covered iron weights are an excellent choice. But these high-tech beauties have a steep price. Expect to pay at least $1.50 a pound for them.

A good alternative to chrome weights are rubber-covered iron weights. They are extremely quiet, won't mark up your floor, and won't ever rust. Surprisingly, even with their extra padding, they don't take up that much extra room on a barbell. A complete 110-pound set will sell for approximately $125.

If you are serious about your weight lifting and start to move up to heavier weights, you should consider buying an Olympic model barbell and Olympic plates. The holes in the middle of these manhole-size iron plates are a lot wider than those found on standard weights. You can't fit Olympic plates on a standard-size barbell, and you can't fit standard-size plates on an Olympic bar.

An Olympic bar weighs 45 pounds and is 7 feet long. It has a revolving sleeve to rotate the weights on Olympic-style lifting movements such as the clean and jerk. Expect to pay at least $350 for a standard 310-pound Olympic set.

When you buy Olympic plates make sure that the hole in the center of the plate is smoothly ground down, or else it will quickly chew up your expensive bar. Also, make sure that the weights weigh what they're supposed to weigh. It's not uncommon to buy Olympic plates made in the Republic of China (they're either stamped "ROC" or have "Republic of China" painted on the plates) that are marked as weighing 45 pounds when in reality they tip the scales at 38 pounds or less. Don't be embarrassed about bringing a scale with you to the store if you're interested in purchasing Chinese weights!

If you are just starting out with weights, a basic 110-pound iron weight and barbell set is a good way to begin. Expect to pay about $80 for everything. Additional weight plates can be purchased for about 50 cents per pound. Individual weight plates start at 2½ pounds and go up to 100 pounds. If you are serious about your weight training, consider buying an extra barbell, weight plates, and dumbbells. By having two or more bars available and a wide array of plates and dumbbells, you can speed up your workouts considerably by eliminating the time spent changing plates.

Weight Bench

Another basic piece of equipment you'll want for your workouts is a weight bench. Buy one with a sturdy welded weight rack that is wide enough for you to get a good shoulder-width grip on the barbell. Don't buy a bench that makes you feel crowded in when you do your lifts. This creates a dangerous situation that could lead to a muscle-overuse problem, as well as a hazardous lifting position. A taut Naugahyde cover on the bench is best for comfort and long bench life. Good quality benches start at $100 and go up to $400.

Training Tips

MAKE YOUR WEIGHT WORKOUTS WORK FOR YOU

The following simple training tips will help you achieve maximum gains from your weight-training workouts.

1.   Don't try to be Superman and overload your bar or weight machine. By knowing your physical limitations and then trying to work with a carefully monitored program, you will begin to overcome these limitations safely and scientifically. Overexerting yourself can only lead to injury and certain setback to your training.

2.   Proper warm-ups are critical to the success of your program. Running, riding your exercise bike, skipping rope, or using a ski machine or rower are some of the ways to get your heart rate up to your training zone and prepare your muscles for the impending weight work.

3.   Breathe correctly when you lift. The correct way to breathe is to inhale just before you lift and exhale slowly as you let the weights back down.

4.   Have a friend spot for you when you lift heavy free weights. This way you remove all chance of having the weights fall on top of you.

5.   Wear loose-fitting, comfortable clothing. If your shirt or shorts bind or chafe you, you'll never be able to attain proper lifting form.

Weight Workouts

THINK JOINTS BEFORE MUSCLES

I'm sure you think of developing stronger and bigger muscles when it comes to weight work, but this should be the least of your concerns. Your muscles can withstand just about any type of abuse you can give them. Pound them, beat them, overstretch them, do whatever you want to them. After some rest they'll come back good as new. "Your muscles can adapt to all situations," says Andy Glass, a former Golden Gloves boxer, now marketing director for Cybex, the exercise and medical testing equipment company in Ronkonkoma, New York. "It's as if God announced: 'Muscles will be the most adaptive tissue of the body. They will respond to all stress by getting stronger.' "

But your joints are totally different from muscles, and not hurting them is what you should be primarily concerned about in your weight-lifting program. It's essential that the joints be properly conditioned and prepared for any weight-training workout. You do this by warming up and putting your joints through their full range of motion before you even lift a weight. This lubricates the cartilage—the soft (irreplaceable) substance that cushions the ends of bones—with synovial fluid and prepares them for the upcoming overload situations.

WARM-UP

A 5-to15-minute warm-up should include some of the following routines: skipping rope, slow jogging, arm swings, jumping jacks, or side bends. When you're ready to begin your weight work, you should be sweating, feeling loose and ready to lift.

Form and Technique

CHOOSE YOUR WEIGHTS WISELY

If this is your first time with a weight program, or if you've been off your program for a while, experiment with different weights to see how they feel. Finally, when you're ready to begin, choose a weight that seems comfortable for the movement you want to do, then use *half* of that weight. Don't consider yourself a wimp or a sissy for going with the lighter weights. You will be smart, though. In your early workouts you should be working with light weight at 15 reps. This way you'll properly condition your joints without damaging them, you'll be able to learn proper lifting technique with little strain on your joints, and you'll gradually increase your strength and endurance.

BREATHING

It's important that you maintain an easy breathing pattern when you lift weights. As you are about to lift, inhale deeply. This will get the needed oxygen into your system. Exhale as you perform the weight movement. Don't ever hold your breath when you lift weights. By cutting off your oxygen supply and at the same time placing a huge demand on the muscles that are lifting the weights, you could very easily pass out.

FORM

Follow the recommended lifting form presented for each weight-training exercise. Deviating from the proper form will reduce the overload on the muscle group that you want to develop. But, even more important, poor form can lead to injury by overstressing joints and tendons that aren't strong enough to bear the added weight. In most cases poor form comes from trying to lift too much weight or from lifting heavy weight when you are too tired to lift properly. Reduce the weights and do the exercise correctly.

For the best results, lift weights smoothly through your full range of motion. Once you reach the top, *slowly* bring the weights back down to the beginning position. The slower you bring the weights down, the more you will overload and thereby develop the muscles.

Repetitions and Sets

A repetition is the number of times a weight is lifted in a particular exercise. A set is a series of repetitions. Although the number of sets and repetitions recommended for each weight workout have not been clearly established by exercise physiologists, the following is what is generally recommended by most weight and strength coaches.

For muscular toning: 3 sets of 20 or more reps with light to moderate weight.

CIRCUIT TRAINING PROGRAM

Station	Purpose	Duration	Intensity	Equipment Options
aerobic	warm-up	3–5 minutes	60–65% maximum heart rate	bike, rower, ski machine, treadmill
progressive resistance	body-shaping strength	20–25 repetitions[1]	lightweight warm-up	multistation gym, free weights
aerobic	cardiovascular conditioning, weight loss	5–10 minutes[2]	70–85% maximum heart rate	bike, rower, ski machine, treadmill
stomach crunch[3]	abdominal conditioning	20–40 repetitions	to fatigue	mat
progressive resistance[4]	body shaping/strength	10–15 repetitions (2 sets)	choose weight to fatigue	multistation gym, free weights
aerobic[5]	cardiovascular conditioning, weight loss	5–10 minutes	70–85% maximum heart rate	bike, rower, ski machine, treadmill
aerobic	warm-down	3–5 minutes down to 60%	bring heart rate down to 60% maximum	bike, rower, ski machine, treadmill

[1]All progressive resistance stations should be performed at low weight for 20–35 repetitions during the warm-up phase.

[2]I would consider 5 minutes a minimum amount of time during an aerobic station of the circuit. The actual duration should be determined by examining one's goals. (I.e.: If weight loss is a primary goal, more time in the aerobic phase will help in caloric expenditure.) If body shaping is the primary goal, the program should include more emphasis in the progressive resistance area.

[3]Stomach crunches should be done by keeping the lower back in contact with the floor/mat during the activity.

[4]The number of progressive resistance stations should be dictated by one's goals. (E.g.: chest-bench press/ incline presses/flys thighs-leg extension/squat/leg press.

[5]I recommend 3–4 aerobic phases.

For muscular endurance: 3 sets of 10 to 12 reps of moderate to heavy weight.

For muscular strength: 3 sets of 4 to 8 reps of heavy weight.

In your first few weight-training sessions start out with low weight (a weight you can lift with little trouble 10 times; then take half of this weight to begin) for 1 set of 10 repetitions of each exercise. As you begin to feel stronger in ensuing workouts, increase each exercise by 1 repetition at each workout, finally building up to 15 reps per exercise.

Once you plateau at 15 reps, increase the weight by 5 pounds and drop your reps back down to 10. As in the beginning, start to increase your reps, finally building up again to 15 reps per exercise. At this point you are ready to begin 2 sets per exercise. Once you are able to safely complete 2 sets of 15 reps per exercise, increase to 3 sets. Between each set take a 2-to-5-minute rest from lifting. If you have the desire, ride your bike, skip rope, or use your rower, treadmill, or ski machine to get your heart pumping to its training zone.

When you're doing your reps, the early ones shouldn't feel too difficult. It's only as you get over the hump and close in on your final reps that you should start to feel a "burning" in your muscles, an aching feeling that can get so intense you feel as if you can't push, pull, or lift any longer. Don't give up! Suck in your stomach and push on to the last rep. This is how you build muscular strength and endurance!

The overload principle is the basis for all weight-training programs. By lifting, pushing, or pulling more weight than the body is accustomed to, the body will start to adjust to that new overload. When stressed over a period of time, muscle size, endurance, and strength will begin to increase to offset the overload situation.

Once an exercise routine starts to feel easy, you'll know that you've reached a workout plateau and are ready for a new overload. Begin to add more weight in your next workout, remembering to increase the weights by no more than 10 pounds. Adding too much weight can easily lead to muscle fatigue, improper lifting form, and eventually a joint injury that can set your training back considerably.

Weight Workouts

The most basic weight-training exercises work the muscles of the midsection, chest, arms, legs, shoulders, and back. There are many different weight routines and they can yield different results for each person.

Often a particular weight program that works well for a friend does not yield the same results for you; progress has to do with genetics as much as with personal intensity and motivation.

By seeking the advice of a knowledgeable health-club operator, exercise physiologist, or strength coach at a local university, you can effectively sidestep the hit-and-miss approach commonly associated with many home weight-training programs. These professionals have dealt with body types similar to yours. After assessing your strengths and weaknesses, they can help design a specialized training program for you that will take into consideration the muscle groups that need the most attention.

In lieu of a personal strength coach, following are basic weight workout routines for either free weights or weight machines that you can easily incorporate in your home weight-training program.

Arms

Strong arms are needed for every facet of daily life. The following exercises will best develop arm flexors, biceps, and forearm muscles.

CURLS

Hold the bar waist high with your palms facing outward in front of you, shoulder width apart.

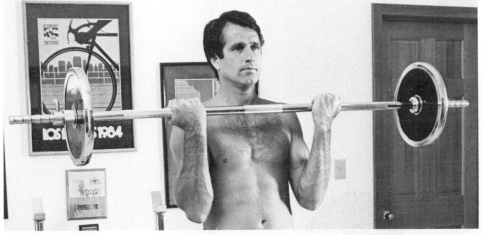

CURLS

Keep your elbows at your sides. Flex your arms at the elbow and start to bring the weights up to your chest in one continuous motion. Keep your back straight and your knees locked. Lower the weights slowly to the beginning position.

WRIST CURLS

Use a swimming kickboard or similar surface to give broad support to your forearms. Place your forearms on the board, palms facing upward.

Let the barbell down at the wrist and then bring it back up again. Repeat.

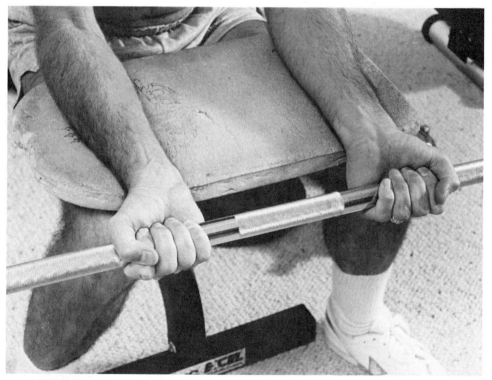

WRIST CURLS

Shoulders

Shoulder strength is important for pushing, pulling, and throwing movements, as well as for raising and lowering the arms. Strong shoulders will stabilize the arms so that they can work more efficiently.

LATERAL RAISES

Hold a dumbbell in each hand, palms facing your thighs.

Raise the weights out slowly until they are slightly above shoulder height. Bring down slowly and repeat.

LATERAL RAISES

MILITARY PRESS

Grasp the bar with the hands shoulder width apart, palms facing inward. Raise to shoulder height. Knees are locked, back straight.

MILITARY PRESS

Push the weights up above your head without bending your back. Arms should be fully extended. Lower the weights slowly back to shoulders and repeat movement.

Midsection

Think of your midsection as a stabilizer. Every time you lift, bend, run, or pull, a strong abdomen constricts to hold you and keep you balanced. A weak midsection can result in a forward tilting of the pelvis, a decrease in support for your abdominal organs, and a subsequent failure to achieve your full athletic potential. The following exercises will help shore up your weaknesses.

LEG RAISES

Lie on your back on a slant board and grab the weight stand with your hands. Bend your knees slightly.

Bring your legs straight up with your knees still bent until your knees are just in front of your face. Lower your legs slowly and repeat the movement.

LEG RAISES

BARBELL GOOD MORNINGS

Place a barbell across your shoulders behind your neck. Stand straight with your feet shoulder width apart. Flex your knees slightly.

Slowly bend forward until your trunk is parallel to the floor. Keep your stomach muscles flexed as you go down. Go back slowly to the starting point and repeat.

BARBELL GOOD MORNINGS

Chest

The chest area includes the rib cage and the surrounding pectoral muscles. These muscles are the ones that help move the shoulder joints.

BENCH PRESS

Lower the weights to your chest, palms facing away from you, hands shoulder width apart.

Push the bar up over your chest, locking your elbows at the highest position. Lower the weight back down slowly. Do not bend or flex your back when performing this exercise. If you start to strain, lower the poundage. When using heavy weights, use a spotter to assist you.

BENCH PRESS

PULL DOWNS

Grab the lat bar of the weight machine, palms facing away from you.

Pull the bar straight down in front of you, almost to waist level. Slowly let it go back up again.

PULL DOWNS

Back

A group of muscles known as the trunk extensors comprise the back muscles, and their main function is to stabilize your back. Exercises geared to strengthening the large muscles of the lower back will help improve your flexibility—your performance in all sports will therefore improve—as well as protect you from lower-back problems by helping to keep you in an upright posture.

BARBELL POWER CLEAN

Stick your feet under the bar, shoulder width apart. Grasp the bar with your palms facing your shins, shoulder width apart. Keep looking forward.

BARBELL POWER CLEAN

Flex your back muscles and then explode upward. Straighten your legs, keeping your elbows straight. Once you are standing erect, go up on your toes, bend your elbows, and swing the barbell up quickly to your shoulders. Keep your elbows under the bar and rest it on the deltoid muscles at the base of your neck. Return the weights to the floor by reversing the movement. Repeat.

Legs

Leg strength is needed for helping you go from a sitting to a standing position, for walking, running, or climbing, and for any other weight-bearing activity.

LEG CURLS

Lie facedown on the bench with your heels under the leg-curl rollers. Hold the edge of the bench with your hands.

Slowly bring your legs up, bending at the knees as much as possible. Do not arch your back; keep your hips flat on the bench. Lower slowly to the starting position and repeat.

LEG CURLS

BARBELL LUNGE

Place barbell on your shoulders behind your neck. When using heavy weights, use a towel to cushion your neck. Stand erect, your feet shoulder width apart, legs straight.

Bend knees slightly, then take a step forward with one leg. Bend both knees slightly, then return to starting position.

BARBELL LUNGE

Circuit Training Program

Circuit training is one of the best ways to minimize the greatest pitfall associated with home workouts: the boredom that comes from constant repetition of the same activity. Simply by segmenting the workout session into "stations," with a machine or exercise to be performed at each station, you will get much more enjoyment and benefit from your workouts.

Stations used in a circuit program are ones that fit your workout goals. The circuit can be entirely aerobic, or a progressive resistance circuit using just your weight machine. Combining your weight training with some form of aerobic workout is the best way to keep your workout fresh and exciting.

The following is a common example of a basic circuit program combining weight work with aerobic conditioning. Modify it to suit your needs.

Common Injuries

OVERUSE SYNDROME

Overuse syndrome is the nagging affliction of active people that is brought on by overusing a particular part of the body, wearing it down to the point where muscle problems or, worse, tendonitis starts to develop in the shoulder, knee, elbow, hip, or wrist.

If detected early, overuse syndrome can be a minor situation that will respond well to aspirin and rest. However, if you continue to lift weights while suffering joint pain, you can aggravate the situation to the point where prescription medicine and months of rest are the only cure. And then, there's no guarantee that the cure will be permanent.

Pushing oneself past the safety limit, which is easy in weight-training programs because it's such a self-directed activity, increases the risk of developing overuse syndrome and tendonitis, the major manifestation of overuse. Tendonitis is caused by the continuous repetition of the same movement. In severe cases, the tendon—the "cable" that connects the muscle to the bone—is pulled at angles over the ends of bones as you go through a movement, causing it to develop microscopic tears. Swelling develops. Over time, if you continue to exercise, the condition gets progressively worse.

The solution to beneficial and safe weight workouts is to admit to yourself immediately that you feel pain the moment it occurs in your joints. Begin with twice-daily ice treatments of 20 minutes a session and take aspirin to relieve these symptoms. Perhaps the hardest thing to do is take time off from the weight work, but this is the best remedy for the problem. The actual time limit for rest is difficult to gauge, and this is what makes overuse syndrome so frustrating to treat. As you rest, you are forced to sit and glumly watch your fitness gains begin to deteriorate. If you get angry at that prospect and come back to weight lifting too soon, you only risk aggravating the condition even more.

Overuse syndrome should not be a reason for keeping you from other forms of exercise. Although you may have strained a tendon or ligament in one part of your body, this should not prevent you from beginning an alternative exercise program. (see ALTERNATIVES TO MAINTAINING FITNESS WHEN INJURED, p. 219.)

As with all injuries that come as a result of your home exercise, or when you have any questions at all about your physical condition, immediately consult your physician.

Select Equipment

The following companies manufacture quality home weight machines and free weights.

WEIGHT MACHINES

Paramount Fitness Equipment Corporation
6450 East Bandini Bl.
Los Angeles, CA 90040
(800) 421-6242

PARAMOUNT FITNESSMATE

Length: 9'
Width: 4'
Height: 7'
Weight: 170-lb. chrome weight stack; optional 230-lb. weight stack
Cost: $1,595

The Paramount FitnessMate offers six exercise stations to provide both lower and

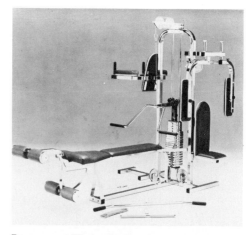

Paramount Fitnessmate

upper body workouts. Renowned for high quality and durability in its line of health-club weight machines, Paramount brings the same workmanship to its home line. The FitnessMate is constructed of 2-inch-square steel tubing and is upholstered in top grade, easy-to-clean Naugahyde that will stand up to years of working out.

Precor USA
PO Box 1018
Redmond, WA 98073
(800) 662-0606

PRECOR 720 INCLINED EXERCISER

Length: 112″
Width: 22″
Height: 55″
Weight: 85 lbs.
Size when folded vertically: 42″ × 22″ × 92″ high
Cost: $500

The 720 is perhaps one of the most versatile pieces of home equipment you could own. It's great for anaerobic workouts and has some aerobic applications as well. Using your own body weight to form the work-load, with this machine you can tone your muscles, improve your flexibility, and extend your endurance while working the various muscle groups through their full range of motion. To operate the 720, simply set height adjustment to one of twenty settings on the monobeam, then sit, kneel, or lie on the glide board to begin one of the thirteen basic exercise routines that you can perform. The big plus with this machine is that because you have full range of motion with your limbs, you can easily invent your own routines and patterns of movement.

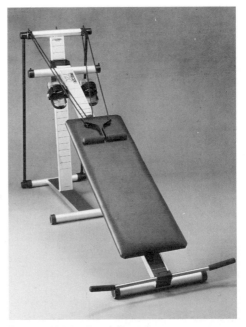

Precor 720 Inclined Exercisor

Universal Gym Equipment Company
Box 1270
Cedar Rapids, IA 52406
(800) 553-7901

UNIVERSAL POWER-PAK 400

Length: 112"
Width: 96"
Height: 84"
Weight: 100-, 180-, or 260-lb. weight stacks
Cost: $2,700

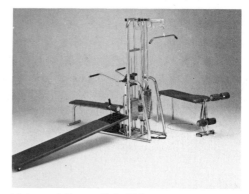

Here's a space-saving home unit that features six separate exercise stations and more than a hundred different exercises. You can set up your own workout routine with this machine, or move from station to station following the recommended routines furnished with each Power-Pak. The Power-Pak 400 is a solid investment and a quality home machine from Universal, one of the most respected names in the weight-machine business.

Universal Power-Pak 400

FREE WEIGHTS

Ivanko Barbell Company
PO box 1470
San Pedro, CA 90733
(213) 514-1155

RUBIMO 110

Cost: $130–$140

Rubber-covered plates are perhaps the most practical idea in free weights for the home. You won't damage your floors, the noise level will be greatly reduced (no more clanking of iron), and the plates won't rust. Ivanko has set high standards in rubber-plated weights with their Rubimo series. The rubber is permanently molded over the cast-iron plates to ensure a lifetime fit. The set comes with a 5-foot solid steel chrome-plated bar; two dumbbells; and graduated plates (four sets of 1¼, 2½, 5, and 10 pounds).

Rubimo 110

York Barbell Company, Inc.
PO Box 1707
York, PA 17405
(717) 767-6481

YORK ARISTOCRAT COMBINATION

Cost: $80

Here's your basic 110-pound starter set of free weights from the official free-weight supplier to the 1984 summer Olympic Games. A 5-foot solid steel bar with chromed sleeve, "wrenchless" collars, 14-inch dumbbells, and graduated plates (four each of 1¼-, 2½-, 5-, and 10-pound plates) make up the set.

York Aristocrat Combination

YORK 190 KILO OLYMPIC INTERNATIONAL BARBELL (with bumper plates)

Cost: $800

Here's over 400 pounds of weight for the serious lifter. Made of the finest alloy steel, these barbells are heat-tempered at York's own foundries. Bumper plates have a 1¼-inch-thick rubber ring bonded to the plate to protect both floors and weights. If you want to pump heavy weights at home, you can't go wrong with this set.

York 190 Kilo Olympic International Barbell (with bumper plates)

YORK MULTI-PURPOSE BENCH

Length: 48"
Width: 9½"
Height: 16"
Weight: 35 lbs.
Cost: $57

This is a basic weight-training bench for bench pressing using the uprights. Made of strong steel tubing, the bench is vinyl covered and well padded.

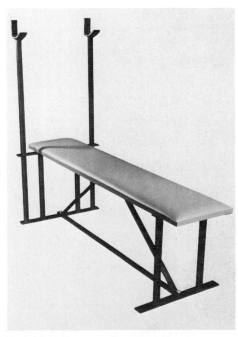

York Multi-Purpose Bench

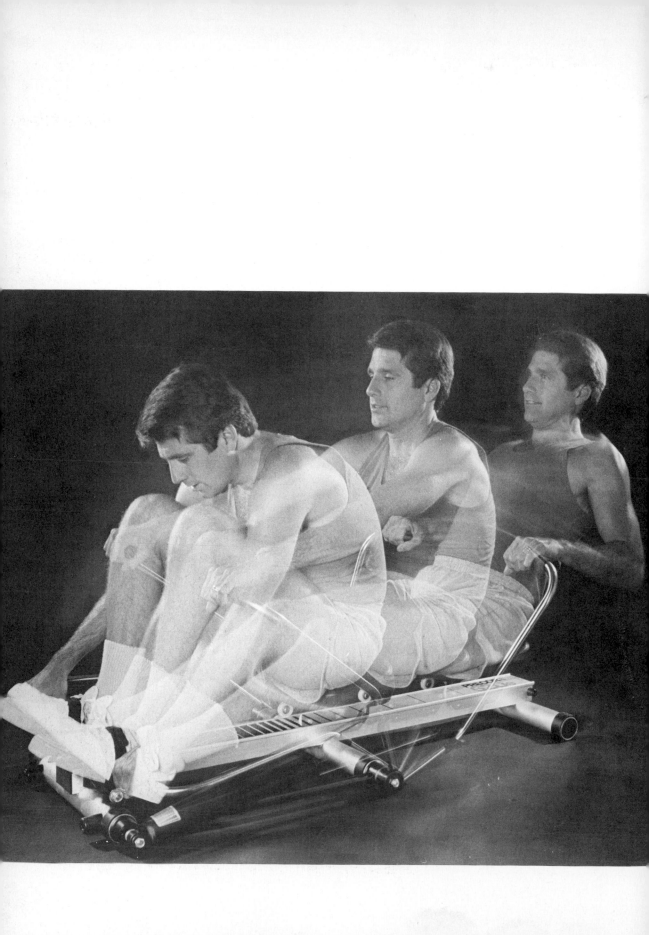

SIX

ROWING MACHINES

Why Row?

At a sportsmedicine symposium held in Seattle shortly before the opening of the 1984 summer Olympic Games in Los Angeles, one of the research papers that was introduced stated that oarsmen (*rowers* to you landlubbers) were the fittest of all athletes at the summer Games. It's easy to understand why. To reach Olympic caliber, most successful rowing coaches agree that a person beginning at age seventeen has to invest 2,000 hours a year in training (out of a possible 8,760 total hours in a year) for five years. Training to earn a seat in an international crew shell means running, lifting weights, and then actually getting in a shell and rowing for an hour or more every day.

When the fitness news concerning rowers was made public, it was not lost to the home exerciser who was searching for the "perfect" exercise, that all-in-one piece that would enhance aerobic conditioning and build muscles in the legs and upper torso as well. Rowing machines virtually walked out of stores in the next few weeks. According to the National Sporting Goods Association, rowing machines now account for

$146.5 million in annual sales (out of $1.5 billion for the entire home-fitness market) and sales are growing steadily each year.

Rowing is a great over-all conditioner. Using a rowing machine regularly three times a week for 20 to 45 minutes is an excellent way to build aerobic conditioning and sculpt your entire body at the same time. Since you are pulling on oars that can be set at a full range of resistances, rowing will exercise and effectively strengthen your back, shoulder, arm, and stomach muscles. And because all rowing machines have movable seats, you are able to exercise your legs as well. Every stroke you take on the rowing machine stretches your calves, hamstrings, and quadriceps in addition to the muscles of your back and arms. All body muscles contract on the drive portion of the stroke and then rest on the recovery portion of the stroke. This way you build and tone your body as you slide your way to fitness.

Rowing is a great calorie burner. Depending on your skill and workout intensity you can burn between 7 and 14 calories a minute. This is almost equal to cross-country skiing, the other total-body exercise, and ranks rowing right at the top among the most physiologically demanding of all aerobic exercises.

"Because you are using so many muscles as you row, you really get your heart rate up fast," says Peter Gardner, the crew coach at Dartmouth College in Hanover, New Hampshire. "Just make sure that you don't get it up too high and tire yourself out too quickly before getting any aerobic benefit from the workout. Unfortunately, it's a mistake that most novices make."

"Rowing is an excellent strength, power, and flexibility builder," says Dr. Larry Klecatsky, a Pelham Manor, New York, resident and an eight-time U.S. National Rowing Team member for the New York Athletic Club as well as a 1976 Olympic team member. "The joint and muscle complaints usually heard from people who run or jog for their exercise aren't heard from oarsmen because rowing is a weight-neutral sport and is done sitting down. Since you are supported by a sliding seat as you exercise, you suffer hardly any of the wear and tear associated with most other legs-only exercises. That's why rowing is such a nice sport."

Who Rows?

Rowing is a total-body exercise that is good for men and women of all ages. A regular program of rowing three times a week for 20 to 45 minutes will tone and strengthen the muscles of your back, stomach, legs, shoulders, and arms. Rowing does have one drawback, however. If you are one of the several million Americans suffering from back problems, you may find that the rowing motion and its stresses may aggravate or worsen your back condition. Therefore, as with all types of home exercise, check with your physician before beginning a rowing program.

If you are in good physical condition and learn to use the rowing machine properly, you can get a very satisfactory workout. According to Tom Cirucci of Universal Fitness Products in Plainview, New York, people who fall in the 25–45-year-old age group generally find rowing machines to be a fine exercise piece and get excellent workouts from them. It's the older people, says Cirucci, who tend to shy away from home rowing, or if they do start, they abandon it very quickly.

"Rowing makes great use of the lower body," Cirucci explains, "and older people generally have little abdominal strength. Rowing really taxes the stomach muscles. Rowing also requires power from the legs and arms. Again, because the older exerciser, especially someone just starting a program, is generally less fit than a younger person, a rowing machine seems more like work than exercise. Since these people receive so little pleasure in working out, they stow the rower in their closet or under the bed and never take it out again."

Rowing can be an exhilarating as well as a physically challenging home exercise. But rowing isn't for everyone. If you have any doubts about whether you'd like to use a rowing machine for exercise, your best bet is first to try one out in a store before buying one. I don't mean just going for a few pulls on the rower, either. Try the machine for a full 5 minutes. Work up a sweat. After testing several machines, if you don't think you'd really be able to get full benefit from the $300-plus machines, perhaps an exercise bike or a cross-country ski machine might be a more suitable purchase for you.

What to Look For in a Rowing Machine

Components

TRACK

When you go to your sports store to try out various rowers, one of the critical points to check is the smoothness of the track. The track is the long bar that the seat slides along. Sit on the seat, fasten the foot straps, and, without pulling on the oars, extend your legs and push all the way back on the track. Do this several times. If your legs can extend fully without the seat hitting the stopper at the end of the track, the machine fits you.

There are several questions you have to ask yourself as you slide back and forth. When you moved in the seat along the track, was it a smooth movement? Did the seat feel locked firmly into the track, or did it slide from side to side? Since you will be sliding back and forth 800 times or more in a half-hour workout, you want a quality track that will give a consistently smooth movement. Anything less—a nick or an imperfection on the track or the rollers under the seat—and you'll be fighting your machine in every workout, and that's something you don't want to do.

FRAME

Look for a machine in the 30–35-pound range. Anything less is not recommended. The major problem with rowing machines lighter than this is that they won't remain stable on the ground as you pull back on the oars. I've tried some of the less-expensive lighter machines and actually jerked the front end of the machine right off the floor as I pulled at high resistance with my drive.

The frame itself should be constructed of anodized aluminum, a metal with an excellent weight-to-strength ratio. This light metal is also quite impervious to the ravages of sweat, something you'll certainly be seeing a lot of once you start a rowing workout.

PISTONS

"Generally, a good sign of a quality rowing machine," says Barry Lynn, a leading fitness consultant based in New York City, "is the size of the pistons on the rowing machine." The pistons provide the resistance you will be pulling against with the oars. Good machines have pistons with a range of 10 pounds of resistance per oar on the low end, and 300 pounds per oar once you switch up to the Superman resistance level at the high end.

On American rowing machines, these pistons are actually Gabriel automobile shock absorbers. The shocks are filled with oil, and when you pull back on the oars, the oil inside the cylinders is squeezed through a small hole, allowing the "oar" to move. To give the smoothest stroke possible and to keep the resistance level uniform throughout the stroke, quality rowing machines will have "gas assisted" pistons. A small sack of Freon is placed in the cylinder to keep air bubbles from forming in the oil, thereby keeping resistance constant and the heat level down.

The degree of heat buildup in the pistons is another factor that separates a good rower from a great one. On most low-end models the pistons will heat up like minifurnaces after just 10 minutes or less of rowing. Don't touch them or you could actually scald yourself. Better yet, stay clear of a cheap rower and you won't have the problem. The pistons on inexpensively made rowers are generally the first major piece that breaks. When this happens, you're most likely out of luck if you want to get it fixed. Don't expect your department store to send back to Taiwan for a replacement part.

Precor USA is a home exercise equipment company whose advanced technology has taken the shocks used in their rowing machines one step further than anyone else. Precor uses an exclusive patented Ventrika valving system on all of their rowers, which keeps the resistance constant no matter how hard or how long your rowing workout is. Heat buildup is also kept to a minimum. Once again, this is an example of how a high-tech company gives you a repeatable, rhythmic, and constant home workout *without* the hassles of battling with your machine.

Stay away from rowing machines that come with air-bladder pistons. These cylinders work like bicycle-tire pumps, and when the bladder on the inside dries out—which is *not* uncommon—you lose evenness in your strokes and eventually all resistance on the oars. Row this one out to the trash pile!

ROWER ARMS

To set resistance on your rowing machine, you have only to turn a knob on each of the rower arms or in the case of the Concept II, move the chain. This changes the angle of leverage on the rods that join the rower to the piston, making the oars harder or easier to pull back. The biggest problem that I've encountered with setting resistance on most rowers is that it's not easy to see the notches etched in each of the rowing arms—if any are even etched in. This will invariably cause you to set the resistance level on the two arms inaccurately, with the end result being a frustrating, imbalanced row. To date, only Precor USA rowing machines come with easy-to-see notches etched deeply in black on the rowing arm, which is certainly a big plus for someone who wants to change resistance settings quickly throughout a workout.

For the resistance knobs, look for heavy-duty plastic clamps. Unlike metal knobs, the plastic ones won't scratch or break and will hold up at heavy resistance.

Also, check the hand grips. Many rowing machines come only with molded plastic grips. After just a short while of pulling on these grips, you'll be looking for a pair of padded cycling gloves. Better rowing machines have thick foam padding on the grips. They won't get slippery when you start to pull and they'll keep your hands from developing blisters.

SEAT

The seat should be contoured and well padded to support your pelvis and spine. Make sure that the seat glides easily with you on it along the full length of the track. The more rollers under the seat, the smoother the ride. Be sure the seat doesn't shimmy from side to side as it moves along, or snag on any part of the track.

FOOT PLATE

On a quality rower your feet will sit in individual pivoting foot plates. The straps that hold your feet in place should be wide, comfortable, long enough, and have Velcro closures to ensure an easily adjustable and snug fit.

PORTABILITY

None of the rowing units comes with transport wheels, but since the units generally weigh only about 40 pounds, you should be able to move them without too much trouble. For ease of storage, many rowers can be stood vertically when not in use. Check for that feature on your rower, especially if you plan to put it away in a closet or stand it against a wall after each workout.

Rowing Machines and the Rowing "Feel"

If you are a serious oarsman or have dreams of becoming one, don't expect to get a similar stroke motion from a home rowing unit as you would from a custom racing shell. The rowing motion in a shell, where you have to lift, bend, and "feather" the oar, is quite different from what you do on a portable rowing machine. The rowing arms on your home "shell" move only in a simple horizontal plane, backward and forward. This may be fine for a home exerciser whose only aim is aerobic exercise. But if you want to duplicate the actual rowing motion, you should seriously consider the next best thing to being on the water: the Concept II Rowing Ergometer.

"This is what oarsmen prefer to use off the water," says Steve Kiesling, an editor at *American Health* magazine and a member of the 1980 Olympic rowing team. *The Shell Game,* his excellent book pub-

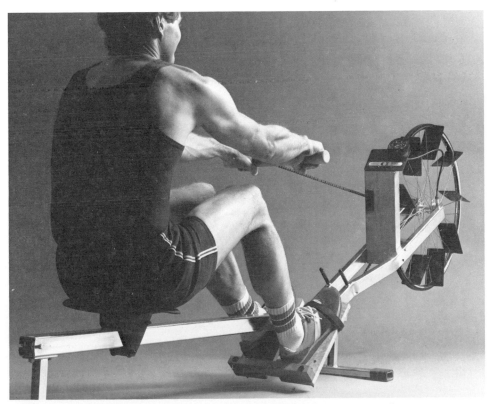

If you're serious about your rowing and can't get out on the water, the Concept II Rowing Ergometer is a great substitute. Just be sure you have the space for it in your house or apartment.

lished in 1982, is a chronicle of his training leading up to the games, and is certainly one of the most enlightening looks at the international rowing scene and what it takes for an athlete to get there. Kiesling still keeps his 8-foot Concept II in his New York apartment. Crimped for training time because of his job, he did the bulk of his training for the 1984 Olympic rowing trials right in his living room.

"With the large wheel out front pulling air in as you stroke back, the Concept II accurately duplicates the feel of a scull moving through water," says Kiesling. "Plus, the machine is so large that it never lets you forget if you've forgotten or missed a workout. It's always there like a silent reminder."

The first company to use the radical Concept II rower design and theory of using a large front wheel to provide resistance is AMF which developed the Benchmark 920 rower. Created by industrial designer Andrew Kostanecki, the 920 is a remarkably handsome machine that also gives the "rowing feel."

"The catch on the 920 is real tough, just like being in a shell," says Mac Good, an oarsman for the New York Athletic Club and founder/director of the Mid Westchester Nautilus in Briarcliff Manor, New York, a club that uses the 920 exclusively for all warm-up routines. "As the front wheel starts to slow down, you have to start it spinning up again," says Good. "It's so much like actual rowing that the only thing missing is water."

How Much You Should Spend

A quality rower will cost at least $300. Once again, you pay for what you get. Add-ons to make your workout more interesting are available and will quickly raise the price of a basic rowing unit. Some bells and whistles that you might want on your rower include a pulse meter to monitor your target heart zone; a clock to keep track of elapsed time and help you during interval work; a stroke counter; and a calorie counter to measure how many calories you burn per minute and for the entire workout.

Add-ons such as these can bring the basic sticker price of your rower up to $600 or more. Again, as with all home exercise machines, add-ons can certainly help motivate you by giving you important feed-back concerning your workout. You just have to decide what your basic needs are to get the best possible workout and then make your purchase accordingly.

Form and Technique

The rowing motion consists of two movements, the *drive* and the *recovery*. In order to achieve satisfactory results and smooth rhythm from your rowing machine, maintaining proper form throughout the two phases of the stroke is important. By acquiring a certain degree of coordination of your legs, stomach, back, shoulders, and arms, your movements will become nonstop and rhythmical.

THE DRIVE

- To begin: Sit on the seat and strap your feet onto the foot plates.
- To start the drive, reach forward with knees bent and grip the oars firmly. Extend your arms straight out, your upper torso bent 45° forward at the waist, depending on how flexible you are. A common mistake is to sit straight up, thereby losing all benefit of your back and stomach power. Good oarsmen get rhythm by leaning forward and sliding up, using their back.
- Fill your lungs with air. Push off with your legs and lean back. Your legs and back will do practically all of the work in this movement. You should be exhaling throughout this entire motion.
- By the time you are halfway through the drive, your legs and back are still doing the work. Your arms should still be straight and your shoulders relaxed.

THE DRIVE, Step 1

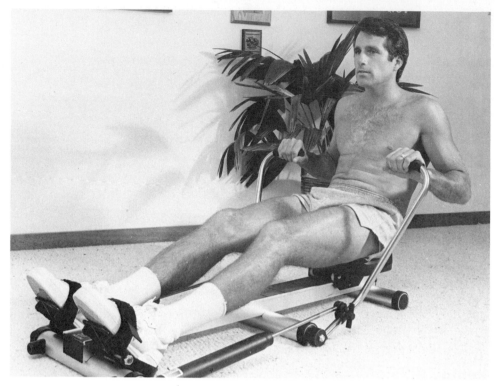

THE DRIVE, Step 2

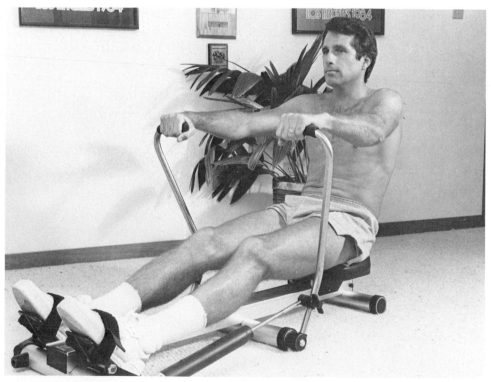

THE DRIVE, Step 3

- Keep your hands level throughout the entire movement.
- At the finish of the drive, your legs should be straight out and your back leaning backward only *slightly*. Pull the oars with your arms and shoulders up to your abdomen.

A common mistake for beginners is to lean too far backward in an effort to pull the oars toward their stomach. This is caused by having the resistance set at too high a level for the arms to bear. Remember, each stroke should be one continuous motion, with no hesitation, straining, or jerking to pull the oars back. If you suffer from any of these problems, lower the resistance until your strength increases. Your initial aim as a beginner, after a few weeks of rowing, is to be able to go nonstop for at least 20 minutes. Only by setting the resistance at a level you can accommodate will this happen.

THE RECOVERY

The recovery begins by extending the arms and swinging the upper body forward at the hips. This pushes the rowing arms forward and

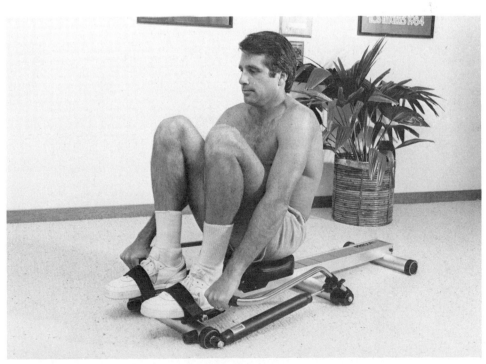

THE RECOVERY

avoids interference between the knees and hands as you pull yourself forward on the seat.

Your body is now back at the original starting position, ready for the next stroke.

Rowing Workouts

When it comes to rowing machines, beginners, especially those from the "No pain, no gain" school of exercise, will often forget the basic aerobic tenets and automatically set the resistance levels too high. Once they do this, they are forced to grunt and groan as they struggle to pull back on the oars. This quickly brings them into an anaerobic phase where they're short on oxygen, gasping for breath, and forced to stop their workouts prematurely. *Remember*: To achieve cardiovascular endurance on your rowing machine, you have to perform hundreds of repetitions during your workout at only *moderate,* yet *continuous,* resistance.

Rowing Workouts

There are two basic ways of working out on a rowing machine—either rowing long steady distance or rowing intervals. "In LSD, or steady-state rowing, your aim is to set the machine at fairly light loads," recommends Peter Gardner, the crew coach at Dartmouth College. "You want to be able to row for at least twenty minutes or longer without exhausting yourself. LSD workouts burn a lot of fat stores in addition to building up your endurance, which makes these workouts perfect for out-of-shape beginners."

Intervals on a rowing machine can be completed in different ways. One way is to row a set of very fast strokes, followed by a set of much slower strokes. Another popular way is to row almost to your maximum heart rate for a set period of time (1 minute, for example), then slacken off for another set period of time (2 or 3 minutes). Then, too, you can row intervals by using a pulse meter. Row hard at 150 bpm for 2 or 3 minutes, then cut back on the strokes until your pulse drops down to 95 bpm before starting out again.

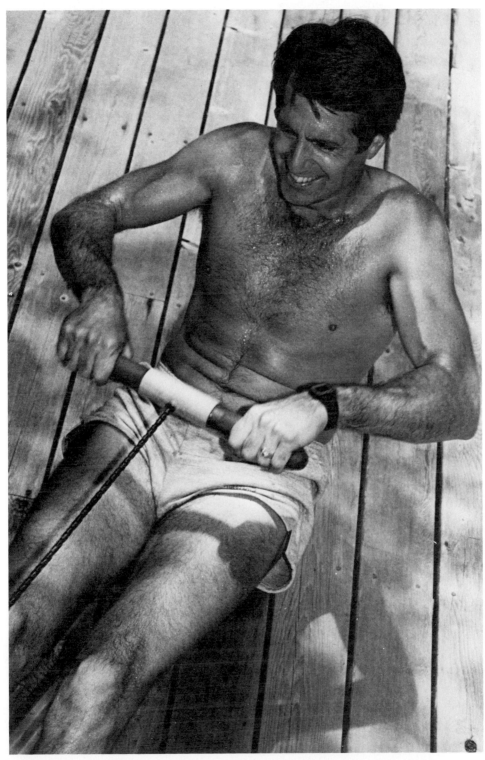

In the middle of a long, hard set.

BEGINNER

To begin a rowing program, as in all home gym workouts, you will have to build up your strength, flexibility, and aerobic endurance through LSD training. Trying to move up too fast over your present conditioning level will be counterproductive and could set your training back through muscle pulls, strains, or joint damage. It's also tough on the psyche to pull and strain on the rower and feel yourself making absolutely no progress.

Warning: Rowing uses most of the muscles in your upper and lower back. The more sedentary you are, the more prone you will be to the effects of rowing on your back muscles. If you have a bad back, or haven't done any type of exercise for more than a year, or if you think that rowing will pose any type of physical strain for you, consult your physician before starting out.

WORKOUT 1

Total time: 15 minutes
Target heart rate: 50–60 percent of maximum heart rate

The aim of this beginning session is to acquaint you with your rowing machine. Sit on the seat, strap in your feet, and start out without using the rowing arms. Simply glide backward and forward on the track for several minutes. This will get your ankle, knee, and hip joints warmed up as well as teach you how to push off with your legs on the drive, and pull back with your stomach muscles on the recovery part of the stroke.

Try the oars now. Experiment with several resistances or speeds (in the case of the Concept II), and get a feel for them. See how hard it is to pull at maximum resistance or speed and how easy it is at low resistance. Stay with low and intermediate resistance speed levels for the next few weeks. There is no need to go into the high-resistance power range. Your aim in upcoming sessions is to methodically build up the time you are able to exercise on this machine at the prescribed heart rate. This accumulated time and low-level intensity will burn off body fat and effectively build your aerobic base.

WORKOUT 2

LSD

Total time: 20–30 minutes, three times weekly
Target heart rate: 60–65 percent of maximum heart rate

This is a workout for someone who has been rowing for at least a few weeks.

5–10 minutes: Warm up at low resistance.
10–15 minutes: Workout consists of rowing at a slightly higher resistance, keeping within the lower end of your target heart rate. In ensuing weeks, increase the length of time spent rowing in each workout in 1-minute increments.
5 minutes: Cool down with easy rowing at little or no resistance.

WORKOUT 3

INTERVALS

Total time: 25–35 minutes, twice weekly
Target heart rate: 65–75 percent of maximum heart rate

5–10 minutes: Warm up at low resistance.
15–20 minutes: Increase resistance and row fast and rhythmically for 30 seconds, keeping at lower end of target heart rate. After 90 seconds or more of rest, rowing with little or no resistance at all, start up again. Do 5 repetitions.
5–10 minutes: Cool down with little resistance.

INTERMEDIATE

You should easily be able to row a half hour nonstop before attempting the following workouts.

WORKOUT 1

LADDERS

Total time: 25–40 minutes
Target heart rate: 70 percent of maximum heart rate

5–10 minutes: Warm up at low resistance.
15–20 minutes: Increase resistance slightly, then row 10 strokes fast, 20 strokes easy; 20 strokes fast, 20 strokes easy; 30 strokes fast, 20 easy. When you get up to 50 or more strokes fast, start working your way back down the ladder to the starting point.
5–10 minutes: Cool down at low resistance.

WORKOUT 2

INTERVALS

Total time: 30–40 minutes
Target heart rate: 75–80 percent of maximum heart rate

5–10 minutes: Warm up at easy resistance.
20 minutes: Increase resistance. Use your heart rate as an indicator of proper resistance. Row nonstop for 3 minutes, then take a 1-minute rest interval with low or no resistance. Do 5 reps. In each succeeding week add 1 rep until you get up to 10 reps per session.
5–10 minutes: Cool down at little or no resistance.

WORKOUT 3

TIME TRIAL

Total time: 35–50 minutes
Target heart rate: 75 percent of maximum heart rate

10 minutes: Warm up at low resistance.

Gliding into port after a tough workout.

20–30 minutes: Select either the number of strokes or the distance you want to row. Use a resistance setting that won't put you into the anaerobic zone but will allow you to row smoothly and steadily. Row the piece and record your time as well as number of strokes. Note the improvement over previous time trials.
5–10 minutes: Cool down at low resistance.

ADVANCED

WORKOUT 1

POPPERS

Total time: 30–40 minutes
Target heart rate: 85 percent of maximum heart rate

Poppers are tough exertions that build strength and power by pushing you to your anaerobic boundary, but not over into it. Since poppers place a great strain on your muscles, don't do them two days in a row or more than three times a week.

5–10 minutes: Warm up at low resistance.
20 minutes: Increase resistance to a level higher than the one you normally use. Row fast for 15 seconds. Either count to yourself or check your stroke counter to see how many strokes you did. Because the first rep is a good indicator of your current strength, let this number of strokes be your guide for ensuing reps.

Do 10 15-second poppers (trying to row the same number of strokes you did in the first rep) with a 75-second rest period after each rep.
5–10 minutes: Cool down at low resistance.

WORKOUT 2

INTERVALS

Total time: 25–40 minutes
Target heart rate: 75–85 percent of maximum heart rate

5–10 minutes: Warm-up at low resistance.
15–20 minutes: Increase resistance. Row fast for 30 seconds. Take a

1-minute rest or let your heart rate drop to a predetermined level before starting off again. Do 10 to 15 reps. If you're in better condition, lower the rest interval to 30 seconds.
5–10 minutes: Cool down at low resistance.

WORKOUT 3

TIME TRIAL

Total time: 30–40 minutes
Target heart rate: 75–80 percent of maximum heart rate

5–10 minutes: Warm up at low resistance.
20 minutes: Select either the number of strokes per minute or the distance that you are going to row. Set resistance to a level that will keep you exercising aerobically, and start to row. Keep your form throughout. If you start to tire toward the end and find it difficult to keep up the pace, lower the resistance and keep on rowing.
5–10 minutes: Cool down at low resistance.

WORKOUT 4

LADDER

Total time: 30–45 minutes
Target heart rate: 70–80 percent of maximum heart rate

5–10 minutes: Warm up at light resistance.
20–25 minutes: Set resistance at a moderate level. Row 24 strokes in 1 minute, then ease off for 30 seconds; row 26 strokes in 1 minute, then ease off for 30 seconds; row 28 strokes in 1 minute, then ease off for 30 seconds; row 30 strokes in 1 minute, then ease off for 30 seconds; row 34 strokes in 1 minute, then ease off for 30 seconds. Work your way up as high as you want with strokes, then work your way back down the ladder to the beginning. Do several reps.
5–10 minutes: Cool down at low resistance.

Common Medical Problems

Rowing can be a stressful activity, and since it utilizes the muscles of the back, legs, arms, and stomach, it shouldn't be surprising that a body part may sometimes become injured. However, with a proper warm-up and cool-down and by refraining from interval workouts two days in a row, you can protect yourself fairly well from most injuries. Following are two common rowing-related injuries that you might expect.

BLISTERS

Developing blisters on your hands from rowing is not uncommon, even if you've been rowing regularly for weeks without a problem. A blister is a sac of skin that collects fluids after the skin has been persistently rubbed by a piece of equipment, in this case the oar handle. What happens is that the friction causes the outer skin layers to separate, thereby allowing fluid to seep in and fill the space.

Blisters will heal faster when the fluid is drained. First, clean the area thoroughly either with soap and water or with alcohol. Sterilize a sewing needle with a match; once it cools sufficiently, prick the edges of the blister and force the fluid out. Leave the skin flap covering the blister because this will provide a natural protective covering while the inflamed area heals underneath. Dry the area completely and cover it with a bandage.

Blisters on your hands can be prevented by wearing cycling or lightweight gardening gloves as you row. Once you develop calluses on your palms, you can remove the gloves. Try to keep your palms dry when you row.

MUSCLE PULL

When a muscle pull occurs during rowing, it is generally because you haven't properly warmed up prior to your workout. What then happens is that you exert more pressure on your muscles, especially those of the arms, than they are prepared to handle. Muscle fiber then begins to pull away from the muscle and you instantly feel pain. In severe cases, muscle actually pulls away from the tendon, and you feel excruciating pain. In both cases, stop rowing immediately. If you try to continue, you will only cause more damage to the muscle. You can't will the pain away.

Treatment for a muscle pull is always the same four-part program applicable to most home exercise injuries: rest, ice, compression, and elevation, or RICE as it's more commonly called (see RICE, p. 215).

Rest: Once you are injured, don't continue with your workout. Take a break until you are once again pain free. Continuing to exercise will only aggravate the condition.

Ice: Ice down the injury with an ice pack for up to 20 minutes at a time. This keeps the broken blood vessels from bleeding and causing the muscle to swell.

Compression: Compress the injured part with an elastic support bandage to reduce swelling and possible strain.

Elevation: Whenever possible, elevate the injured area above the level of the heart to help reduce swelling.

Once the pain has gone away, start weight training exercises to bring the damaged muscle back to normal strength. You can go back to your rowing, but refrain from any type of heavy-resistance work until you can easily handle LSD workouts without feeling any tightness, strain, or weakness in the muscle.

Select Equipment

Following are some of the quality rowers now on the market that will give you excellent value and good workouts.

AMF American
200 American Ave.
Jefferson, IA 50129
(800) 247-3978

BENCHMARK 920

Length: 82.5″
Width: 25″
Height: 15″
Weight: 79 lbs.
Cost: $595

The 920 is one of the two home rowing machines currently available that simulate the actual rowing feel. Part of AMF's Benchmark series of home exercise equipment, the 920 is fully electronic and comes with twenty different resistance settings, which are regulated with a simple press of your finger. The 920 has a pull strap in place of

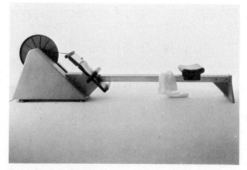
Benchmark 920

oars that connects to an electromagnetic resistance system. The electronic control panel gives liquid crystal display (LCD) readouts of time, calories burned, and resistance. The unit plugs into a standard wall outlet.

Concept II, Inc.
RR 1, Box 1100
Morrisville, VT 05661-9727
(802) 888-4404

CONCEPT II ROWING ERGOMETER

Length: 100"
Width: 18"
Height: 34"
Weight: 65 lbs.
Cost: $600

Concept II Rowing Ergometer

The Concept II is a rower for someone who wants a superb rowing workout and has the space in his home for this extra-long machine. The spinning flywheel in front pulls in air and provides resistance. The harder and faster you pull, the more resistance you get. Resistance is also altered simply by moving the drive chain to another sprocket on the wheel. A speed-ometer/odometer measures the speed and distance of the flywheel. Because of the spoked flywheel, the machine could be dangerous in a home setting with young, curious children. Available only direct from the factory.

MONARK
Universal Fitness Products Company
20 Terminal Drive South
Plainview, NY 11803
(516) 349-8600

MONARK 633 ROWER

Length: 56"
Width: 22"
Height: 8"
Weight: 41 lbs.
Cost: $325

Monark 633 Rower

This is a quality rower from Monark, a respected name in home fitness equipment. The 633 has easy-to-adjust resistance levels at ten different settings, hydraulic pistons, and a stabilizer bar in the middle of the track to keep the unit securely on the floor as you go through your workout.

M & R Industries, Inc.
9215 151st Ave. NE
Redmond, WA 98052
(800) 222-9995

AVITA 950 PROFESSIONAL ROWER

Length: 49"
Width: 30"
Height: 9.5"
Weight: 41 lbs.
Cost: $350

This is AVITA's top-of-the-line rower. It comes with a five-year warranty on the frame and a one-year warranty on materials and workmanship. Resistance is from computer-matched, gas-assisted cylinders and sealed ball-bearing oar pivots.

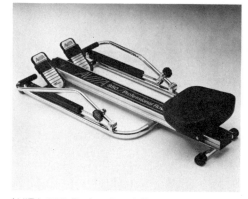

AVITA 950 Professional Rower

Precor USA
Box 1018
Redmond, WA 98073
(800) 662-0606

PRECOR 620e DUAL PISTON PROFESSIONAL ROWING MACHINE

Length: 53"
Width: 32"
Height: 11"
Weight: 44 lbs.
Cost: $395

The 620e is a sturdy unit complete with stroke counter, oil-filled hydraulic cylinders, and stabilizer bar. Your work load is conveniently set with microadjust knobs on each rowing arm.

Precor 620e Dual Piston
Professional Rowing Machine

PRECOR 630e ROWING ERGOMETER

Length: 51"
Width: 30"
Height: 9"
Weight: 43 lbs.
Cost: $575

Pop in the 9-volt battery and the 630e is ready to row. Microprocessor-controlled electronics give accurate readings of elapsed time, stroke rate, total strokes, work rate in calories burned per minute, and total caloric expenditure.

Precor 620e Rowing Ergometer

SEVEN

TREADMILLS

Why Run?

Walking and, as your fitness level improves, running on a treadmill are two quick routes to cardiovascular fitness. Using a treadmill three or four times a week for 20 to 45 minutes within your target heart zone is an excellent workout for the heart and lungs. Treadmill running is also excellent for the muscles of the lower body, especially the hamstrings and calf muscles in the backs of the legs. A regular treadmill program will help lower your blood pressure, increase your heart's ability to pump more blood with less effort, increase your high-density lipoprotein cholesterol count (the "good cholesterol"), and burn off body fat.

Treadmills certainly belong in a home gym. Serious runners can use their motorized treadmills whenever they want to work on their training program as well as their running form. And those of you who love to run but are just too bashful to be seen in public or, worse, don't have time to go out for a run, you can now run in the privacy of your home whenever you want. Finally, with a treadmill in place, gone are the excuses of not being able to put in the miles or the time. If you commit yourself to your treadmill-exercise regime as you would to a business appointment, you'll achieve and maintain fitness results in a very short period of time.

Motorized and NonMotorized Treadmills

There are two types of treadmills on the market today: those that have motors and those that don't. If your exercise program is going to consist solely of walking, I recommend purchasing a nonmotorized unit. Nonelectric treadmills will give years of service and, because they have so few moving parts, are virtually maintenance free.

If you are more interested in running at a fairly fast pace or want to use the treadmill as a foul-weather training alternative to your outdoor activities, then look into a motorized treadmill. Its faster speed will give a much more satisfying workout than you can get from a nonmotorized one.

As a training device, motorized treadmills have been struggling for the past fifteen years. Their motors and other working parts just couldn't withstand all the pounding. Originally built to be used in exercise labs to test heart function, treadmills moved quickly out of the lab and into the home when some enterprising runners saw what a great workout treadmills could give. Unfortunately, if the treadmill wasn't an institutional model that weighed as much as a baby elephant and made the noise of two eighteen-wheel trucks racing down a highway, the unit was doomed to break down.

Initially, treadmill technology wasn't as sophisticated as it is now. On the early models, every time a foot hit the belt it would stress the motor. This caused a slight delay, or lag, on the belt. Then, when the motor increased its power to compensate for the heavy footstrike, it would cause the belt to surge, slightly jerking the runner's foot from underneath. When very heavy joggers used these early treadmills, the units came quickly to a standstill as the motors burned out from the strain.

This is not the case today. Fortunately for home exercisers, treadmills are reliable, albeit expensive, tools. Motors and other moving parts on the treadmill have been greatly improved. The models recommended here are quiet, smooth operating, and have easy-to-use control features.

Paul Byrne of Concept 90 Fitness Stores in Fort Lauderdale, Florida, uses his electric Precor 935e treadmill every day as his major source of exercise. Byrne, a former 400- and 800-meter runner for the

Colgate University track team, gets in a half-hour run every morning before going off to his 12-hour workday.

"There are a lot of times when I just don't feel like running at all," says Byrne. "But my daily routine is to turn off the alarm clock, get out of bed, put a Bruce Springsteen tape into the Walkman, and set the dial on the treadmill for 4.1 mph. I slowly get lulled into walking fast for 2 minutes. I then gradually move up to 7 mph for 2 minutes and start to jog. Between 8.5 mph and 9.3 mph I actually start to run and keep it up for 25 minutes. I finish off with a walk at 4.1 mph for 3 minutes."

The beauty of the electric treadmill, says Byrne, is that it forces him to exercise even if he's not particularly motivated at the outset.

All motorized treadmills work on the same principle. An electric motor powers the tread belt as you run along on the belt to keep pace. If the belt is moving too slowly for you, you can easily increase the speed on good treadmills simply by turning a knob or pulling a lever on the control panel located at waist level at the front of the machine. If the machine is going too fast for you and you want to stop, just tap the "kill" switch and the belt will stop in its tracks.

Nonmotorized treadmills, especially the ones that come with adjust-

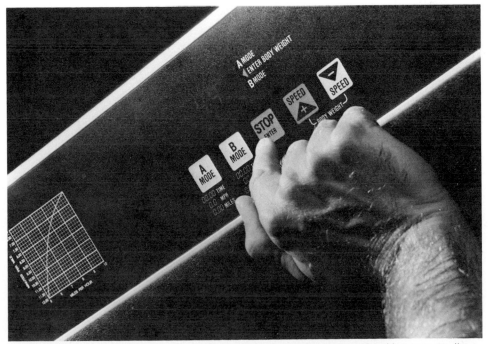

On quality electric treadmills the control panel is just a fingertip away. You can easily increase or decrease speed without losing a stride.

able elevation, are great for people on a prescribed cardiac rehabilitation program where a walking regime is to be their major form of exercise. The machines are less expensive than the motorized models and require little maintenance.

However, these nonmotorized machines aren't for everyone. "I would never recommend a nonmotorized unit to a serious exerciser," says Tom Cirucci of Universal Fitness Products in Plainview, New York. Universal makes the Tredex motorized treadmill. "If you run on a nonmotorized unit your stride gets thrown out of whack because of all the pushing on the treadmill you have to do with your feet. Plus, the rollers hurt your feet, even if you have on thickly padded running shoes. I don't know of anyone who has had a successful running program on nonmotorized models and I actually discourage healthy people from buying one."

What to Look for in a Treadmill

Granted, when you go to a sporting-goods store, the treadmills on display all look snazzy and high tech and it's difficult to tell one from the other. Be careful: this is the time you'll be snagged by a smooth-talking salesperson and possibly sold a bill of goods on a unit that may barely get past 200 miles before it needs an overhaul. To avoid this unpleasantness, following are all the pertinent facts you need to know about treadmills *before* buying one.

Go to the store with your running shoes on. Of all the pieces of home aerobic equipment, the treadmill is the most expensive. You *must* try it before purchasing it; you'll be sorry later if your new and very costly machine doesn't live up to your expectations.

RUNNING SURFACE

Stand next to the machine that interests you and have the salesperson turn it on. Does the running bed rattle and shake? Or does the machine run whisper quiet? What you want to hear from a treadmill is nothing but a gentle hum. There are models like this listed in Select Equipment on p. 162.

Finally, note if the tread belt stays centered on the machine as it's running. Inferior treadmills have wandering belts that will actually start to move from one side to the other. This can be extremely disconcerting when you are running on the machine. You then have to stop the machine, get off, and re-center the belt. In most cases you'll just end your workout right there.

Turn off the treadmill and look closely at the belt. Inexpensive models have thin belts that offer neither foot cushioning nor durability. Make sure the belt on your intended machine is thick and sturdy.

Friction is the enemy of treadmills and causes the most damage to the motor. Every treadmill model except those from Precor USA have to be sprayed regularly with Teflon to lubricate the running bed and keep the belt moving smoothly over it. Friction will eventually shorten the life of the bed, belt, and motor, and that's why you need Teflon spray. If you choose a treadmill that requires regular applications of Teflon or some other lubricant, be sure to follow the manufacturer's recommendation. Treadmills, more than any other piece of home exercise equipment, require the most service, care, and upkeep. Allowing the belt or bed to get dirty is asking for trouble. Expensive trouble.

THE MOTOR

Ask if the treadmill motor is AC or DC driven. Generally, all AC units are quieter, except in the case of the Precor 935 treadmill, a DC unit with a Precor exclusive called "Quiet Kit," which makes the machine as quiet as the best AC driven treadmills.

The most common complaint with most DC units is that there is a lag when your foot hits the belt. This happens because three to five times your body weight comes down on the belt with each footfall. The force of this impact is enough to cause the belt momentarily to slow down, then speed up again once the motor gets an extra surge of power.

This is why you brought your running shoes with you to the store. Get on several treadmills and try them out. On most DC-drive machines the motor does lag slightly when your foot hits. Be aware that this may subtly change your running stride and form.

AC units, on the other hand, are quiet and have no lag on the belt as you run because of the motor's special configuration. A possible drawback, however, is the fact that all AC-driven treadmills use a long vertical lever to change speeds. What you are actually doing when you pull the lever is activating a pulley system that changes the position of the motor and physically moves it to another position.

Be aware that speeds on AC machines start at higher levels than those on DC machines. Also, since you are pulling and moving machinery under the running belt with the vertical speed lever, the risk of breakdown is potentially much higher than on a DC-driven treadmill.

SPECIAL FEATURES

Determine what you'll use your treadmill for. Anyone purchasing an electric model for general fitness use should think about getting a treadmill that has an elevation feature. This way you can add variety to your running workouts. One day you can run hard on a level surface, while the next day you can walk with the treadmill set at a slight elevation. Another time you can run intervals while the treadmill is set at a 15-degree incline. All of this can be controlled with the press of a button to raise or lower the running surface.

Another item that you will want on your treadmill is an easy-to-read and easy-to-reach control panel. Current speed, distance run, calories burned per minute, and total caloric expenditure are some of the control-panel features that will help make your home running program more enjoyable and informative.

How Much You Should Spend

A quality nonmotorized treadmill will cost at least $700, while a good motorized treadmill that has adjustable speed controls will start at $1,200. Higher-priced models in the $2,500–$3,000 range will have extra features such as electric elevation, and a microprocessor to measure calories burned, elapsed time, and distance run. Are costly treadmills for everyone? Admittedly, there are certainly less expensive ways to achieve aerobic fitness at home than by spending a few thousand dollars for a treadmill. Currently, many of the treadmills sold are bought by cardiac-rehab patients who have been told by their physicians to follow a carefully regulated walking/running program using a pulse meter and a treadmill. For these people, to pay a few thousand dollars for a treadmill doesn't seem like an extravagance when they consider their alternatives.

To buy or not to buy a treadmill really comes down to how much use you think you will get out of the unit. An important consideration is if you can afford it.

But take it from me, someone who's run on every type of surface around the globe during the span of an international running career:

Laugh at the bad weather raging outside as you get a great workout running in the comfort of your own home while watching your favorite show.

today's quality treadmills are quiet, efficient, relatively maintenance free, and provide great workouts. If you love to run but for some reason can't find the time or the place to do it, you should seriously consider buying a motorized treadmill. Financing is made available by some treadmill manufacturers. When it's raining, snowing, or hailing outside, you can laugh at the weather. With your own motorized treadmill, it will always be room temperature and miles to go before you sleep.

Getting Ready to Run

If you want to get started on a program using a treadmill, your first priority should be to buy the very best running shoes you can afford. In case you haven't been in a sporting-goods store in the past decade, the days of the $10 all-purpose sport shoe are long gone. Figure on spending between $35 and $100 for a good pair of running shoes. Running-shoe stores—those staffed by runners and catering to the running community—offer good shoe advice and the best shoes. Although the shoes in these stores generally cost slightly more than what you might pay in a department store, you will more than make up the price difference with the expert advice you receive. Salespersons in these stores know from their years of firsthand experience which particular shoe models will be most comfortable and give the most support for your feet and body size.

Following are some tips on what to look for when you buy running shoes.

- The shoe has to be comfortable. Don't be swayed into buying a shoe model because some Olympic gold medalist wears that particular shoe. If the shoes don't feel good on your feet, don't buy them.
- The soles of the shoes shouldn't be too stiff. Take the shoe in your hand and bend it at the midsole. If the sole is too stiff it will prevent your foot from flexing properly on impact, which could lead to shin splints or Achilles tendonitis (see Medical Problems, p. 214).
- Make sure that there is ample cushioning at the ball of the foot. Generally this is where the greatest amount of force is placed on the foot.
- Shoes don't generally loosen up too much after you buy them, so make sure that your toes aren't cramped or pinched. If you buy a pair of tight shoes, I guarantee you'll be suffering from blisters, corns, or calluses after just a few runs on the treadmill.

• Make sure that the heel counter in the shoes—the piece at the back of the shoe—is stiff and holds your foot snugly. If the heel counter isn't stiff enough, your foot will move around inside the shoe as you run, which could lead to an injury that easily could have been avoided.

Form and Technique

I like running on a treadmill after a hectic day. More than any other piece of home equipment, the treadmill lets my mind wander. Psychologists call this disassociating. Free from the hazards of traffic and uneven terrain, I can drift off and think of other things as I put in the miles. Just be careful getting on and off the treadmill. That takes concentration!

Running on a treadmill set at a level setting is a lot easier than running out on the road or on the track. Therefore, it's easier to concentrate on your running form. With no wind resistance to overcome, and with the constant backward movement of the belt aiding in the initial backward thrust of the foot plant, you are free to think more about arm carriage, relaxed shoulders, and stride length.

Although there are no set rules regarding running form, there are certain general principles that will help you run faster, longer, and more efficiently. A biomechanically smooth running form will also help in injury prevention by reducing joint and tendon trauma.

ARMS

Your arms should be in sync with your body as you move. Where you hold them and how fast you move them will ultimately affect not only your stride length and body lean but, in the end, your ability to reach maximum performance.

When you run, avoid flapping your arms or crossing them in front of you. This is a typical mistake made by most beginners, and it makes the upper body rotate and thereby wastes energy. Make sure you're swinging your arms and not twisting your waist; the arms and hands should move forward and back. Your hands should swing easily by your sides, just at the level of your hips.

HANDS

Your hands should be relaxed, not held tightly, when you run. A relaxed hand will result in a relaxed body, which in turn will give you a better running style. Don't clench your fists into tight balls as you run. This will give you a stiff running style.

FEET

Every runner has his own theory of how he should land on his feet. Most people land on the outside portion of their heel. This is perfectly natural and is perhaps the most common form of heel strike. I prefer to land flat, right near midfoot, and then roll forward and push off on my big toe. Landing first on the ball of the foot is not recommended, although there are some marathon racers who claim to run this way with no problems. For the general public, this type of footstrike has a tendency to overstress the bones in the front of the foot, as well as strain the muscles of the calf and the knee. Although sprinters use this type of footstrike almost exclusively, it is less stressful to them because of the short distances they run.

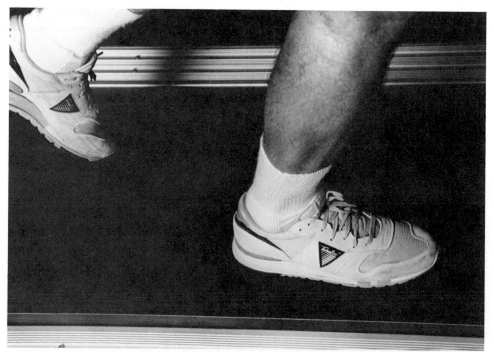

I prefer to land flatfooted, right near midfoot, then roll forward.

POSTURE

Once your foot is on the ground, imagine that there is a straight line running up from your foot, through your hips, and up your back to your shoulders and head. Leaning too far forward past this imaginary line, or too far to the rear, could result in energy loss by minimizing the biomechanic potential of your body. Videotape analysis of top runners has proved this straight-up running style to be the best.

STRIDE

Keep your back straight and maintain form as you run. Don't fall into the trap of thinking that by increasing the length of your stride you will cover more distance faster. You won't. What counts most for joggers regarding stride, and ultimately performance, is the ability to "shuffle" along, moving your legs out at a distance that feels comfortable for you. The ball of your foot should always be directly under the knee when it lands. If you try to stretch out and increase the length of your stride, the ball of your foot will then be way out ahead of the knee when it lands, causing the knee to absorb tremendous road shock. Knee injuries will develop if this overstriding is kept up too long. Remember: If you want to run faster, don't increase your stride length. Increase the number of strides per mile that you take in each running session.

Workout Distances

One of the most important things to remember in starting a running program is to start *slowly.* Have patience and don't try to rush your training. Sure, you are probably thinking "nothing will happen to me if I start out by running a lot of miles." Something surely *will* happen. One of the major causes of injury is that runners, novices especially, take a big jump in their training distances without letting their bodies properly adapt to the changes they have to undergo. A beginner can easily go from a 1-mile workout to 2 miles—a 100 percent jump in distance—within a few weeks after beginning training and most likely not experience an injury. However, should a more experienced runner move up from a steady 5-mile workout to a 10-mile run—again, a 100 percent increase in distance—the risk of injury is very high.

Most orthopedists and coaches agree that when training for competitions, monthly jumps of only 10 percent in mileage are acceptable for a while. Push your mileage past this point and you're asking for muscle pulls, aches, and pains. If you're not training for any race, but are just running for aerobic exercise, and logging more than 15 miles weekly, Dr. Kenneth Cooper of the Aerobics Center in Dallas, says that you're doing more than is actually needed to maintain good health. Recent studies have shown that injuries increase significantly once you start running more than 30 miles per week.

The best guide to how much mileage you should do is how your body reacts to it. An onset of aches and pains should alert you that you're running either too hard or too far.

Whatever your running goals may be—to go outside and compete in a fun run or a local 10-K, or just to maintain over-all fitness—you must keep your training at a consistent level. There's no way you can reach a certain fitness level and then just stop, thinking that your fitness will stay with you even if you don't run. To the contrary. Stop running for as little as six months and you'll lose most of the accrued aerobic benefits and have to start from scratch to work your way back to your former fitness level.

Running Tips

1. If your body is crying out for a break during a treadmill run, the smart thing to do is to give in. You could be setting yourself up for an injury if you push yourself through a workout that you're really not up to doing. Instead, go take a shower. You'll do much better tomorrow. Missing one workout won't ruin your conditioning. Your body is telling you that it needs a rest.

2. Keep track of how many miles you run in each pair of running shoes. Check them frequently for wear on either side of the heel. Also, pay particular attention to the heel counter. After a few hundred miles this will wear out and no longer properly stabilize the foot. If you begin to suffer from unusual leg pains, there's a good chance that your shoes are the cause. It's best to buy two pairs of shoes and alternate their use.

3. For competitive runners, it's a good rule of thumb in training to run at a pace that is a few minutes slower than your 10-K pace. This way you're assured of a consistently fast pace, but not one so fast that it will bring on early fatigue or chronic injury.

4. Of all the aerobic sports you can do in your home gym, running is certainly the most stressful to the body. Listen to your body when it

starts to show signs of fatigue. Don't be afraid to take an extended break from your running. After a layoff, you'll be hungry for a good run and eager to return to the treadmill.

Treadmill Workouts

Treadmills have always been used in physiology labs because the work loads can be monitored more exactly than if the subjects had to run on a track. This is one of the great benefits of running at home on your treadmill. If you want to run exactly a 7:30-mile pace for a half hour, you can do it. When you come back in three days, the weather conditions will be exactly the same and you can repeat your previous workout.

For the beginner, the initial challenge is to stay on the treadmill for 20 minutes at least three times a week. It does not matter if you are walking or running 7-, 9-, or 15-minute miles. The first priority is to get your heart elevated to your target heart rate and keep it there for 20 minutes.

Once you are able to jog for 20 uninterrupted minutes, you can begin to take notice of how fast you are going. In these early stages, constantly remind yourself that it is not how fast you go but how many minutes you can keep running that is important. This is called the long steady distance (LSD) phase of training. LSD running should comprise 90 percent of all the running you will do.

The distance you choose and the time limit you set for yourself in LSD workouts depend on your level of conditioning. But whatever the distance or the time, you should run at a comfortable pace at approximately 70 percent of your maximum heart rate. A good sign of a comfortable pace is whether you are able to carry on a conversation as you run.

The other 10 percent of your running will be comprised of various sprints or faster-tempo running called interval training, or *fartlek,* the Swedish name for "speed play." If you are either a recreational or a competitive runner, the percentage of this speed work is increased proportionately depending on the distance of the race you will be running. For example, a weekly workout consisting of 90 percent LSD and 10 percent speed work is good for a marathoner, while a half-miler will run 50 percent speed work, and a sprinter 90 percent speed work.

For lifelong cardiovascular development, the basic prescription is for 90 percent LSD running. Long steady distance, as a warm-up to other workouts and as a basis for keeping your weight low and providing exercise, is perhaps the most natural and beneficial of all forms of training.

One word of caution: Because a treadmill is so controlled and convenient, it is easy to get on every day and run at the same speed for the same amount of time. But if you do this too much it will cause your running program to stagnate. The body and the mind thrive on different stresses being placed on them. The best way around running the same workouts day after day is try to vary tempo, intensity, and duration. Varying your workouts like this will keep your workouts fresh and exciting and make you look forward to returning again and again.

Treadmill Workouts

The following treadmill workouts constitute a ten-week running sampler geared for the beginner, intermediate, and competitive runner. As with all home-exercise programs, this is only a guide. Feel free to add or delete certain portions of the program depending on your interests, strengths, and weaknesses.

BEGINNER
Target heart rate: 50 percent of maximum heart rate, three days weekly, building up to 60–70 percent MHR by Week 8

Week 1: Walk 20 minutes at a comfortable pace.

Week 2: Walk 5 minutes; jog 5 minutes; walk 2 minutes; jog 5 minutes; walk 5 minutes.

Week 3: Walk 5 minutes; jog 5 minutes; walk 2 minutes; jog 5 minutes; walk 3 minutes.

Week 4: Walk 5 minutes; jog 5 minutes; walk 1 minute; jog 5 minutes; walk 3 minutes.

Week 5: Walk 5 minutes; jog 7 minutes; walk 1 minute; jog 7 minutes; walk 3 minutes.

Week 6: Walk 3 minutes; jog 5 minutes; walk 2 minutes; jog 7 minutes; walk 2 minutes; jog 5 minutes; walk 2 minutes.

Week 7: Walk 3 minutes; jog 7 minutes; walk 1 minute; jog 10 minutes; walk 2 minutes.

Week 8: Walk 3 minutes; jog 15 minutes at a slow pace; walk 2 minutes.

Week 9: Walk 1 minute; jog 18 minutes at same pace as Week 8; walk 2 minutes.

Week 10:

Monday: Walk 1 minute; jog 18 minutes at a slow pace; walk 2 minutes.

Wednesday: Walk 1 minute; jog 15 minutes slightly faster than Monday; walk 2 minutes.

Friday: Walk 1 minute; jog 25 minutes at a slow pace; walk 2 minutes.

INTERMEDIATE (Three times weekly)

Note: At this level you should be able to jog 20 minutes three times a week with no problem. Before each of these workouts, always walk for at least 1 minute as a warm-up and another minute or longer as your cool-down phase.

Week 1:

Monday: Jog for 20 minutes at a good pace at 65 to 70 percent of your maximum heart rate (MHR).

Wednesday: Jog 15 minutes at a faster pace. Target heart rate should be above 70 percent of maximum.

Friday: Jog 22 minutes at a slow pace, keeping your target heart rate at about 60 to 65 percent of maximum.

Week 2: Same as Week 1.

Week 3:

Monday: Jog 20 minutes at 60 to 65 percent MHR.

Wednesday: Jog 10 minutes at 70 percent MHR. Increase pace for 3 minutes, running at 10 percent higher heart rate.

Friday: Jog 20 minutes at 70 percent MHR.

Week 4:

Monday: Jog 20 minutes at 70 percent MHR.

Wednesday: 7 minutes slow-pace jog. Increase the pace and jog faster for 7 minutes. Your heart rate should increase 10 percent; run faster for 3 minutes; jog slowly for 2 minutes.

Friday: Jog 20 minutes at 70 percent MHR.

Week 5: Same as Week 4.

Week 6:

Monday: Jog 20 minutes at 70 percent MHR.

Wednesday: Jog 10 minutes at 70 percent MHR; jog 4 minutes at 80 percent MHR; jog slowly 1 minute; run fast 2 minutes at 80 percent MHR; jog slowly 1 minute; run fast 4 minutes at 70 percent MHR.

Friday: Run 20 minutes at 70 percent MHR.

Week 7: Same as Week 4.

Week 8:

Monday: Run 20 minutes at 70 percent MHR.

Wednesday: Run 5 minutes at 70 percent MHR; run 4 minutes at 80 to 85 percent MHR; jog 1 minute; sprint 2 minutes at 85 percent MHR; run 4 minutes at 70 percent MHR.

Friday: Run 25 minutes at 70 percent MHR.

Week 9:

Monday: Run 5 minutes at 70 percent MHR; run 4 minutes at 80 percent MHR; run 3 minutes at 70 percent MHR; run 2 minutes fast at 80 to 85 percent MHR; run 10 minutes at 70 percent MHR.

Wednesday: Jog 5 minutes at 70 percent MHR; run 1 minute at 85 percent MHR; jog slowly 1 minute at 60 percent MHR; run 3 minutes at 80 percent MHR; jog 2 minutes at 60 percent MHR; run fast for 3 minutes at 80 percent MHR; jog for 3 minutes at 60 percent MHR; jog 7 minutes at 70 percent MHR.

Friday: 5 minute jog at 70 percent MHR; 15 minute jog at 75 percent MHR; 5 minute jog at 70 percent MHR.

Week 10: This is a maintenance week.

Monday: Run 20 to 25 minutes at 70 percent MHR.

Wednesday: Run 5 minutes at 70 percent MHR; run 4 minutes at 80 to 85 percent MHR; jog 1 minute; run fast 3 minutes at 80 to 85 percent MHR; jog slowly 1 minute; run fast 2 minutes at 80 to 85 percent MHR; run 3 minutes at 70 percent MHR.

Friday: Run 15 minutes at 70 percent MHR.

ADVANCED

Week 1: Run 20 to 30 minutes every day at 70 percent MHR.

Week 2: Run 20 to 30 minutes every other day at 70 percent MHR.

Monday, Wednesday, Friday: Throw in a 3-minute interval at 85 percent MHR in the middle of your LSD run.

Week 3: Same as Week 2.

Week 4: Run 20 to 30 minutes at 70 percent MHR on Tuesday, Thursday, Saturday, and Sunday.

Monday: Run 10 minutes at 70 percent MHR; use elevation feature of treadmill and run hard 5 minutes at 85 percent MHR; run 5 minutes at 70 percent MHR.

Wednesday: Run 10 minutes at 70 percent MHR; use elevation on the treadmill and run 7 minutes at 80 to 85 percent MHR; run 5 minutes at 70 percent MHR.

Friday: Run 10 minutes at 70 percent MHR; use elevation and run 10 minutes at 80 to 85 percent MHR; run 10 minutes at 70 percent MHR.

Week 5: Same as Week 4.

Week 6: Run 20 to 30 minutes at 70 percent MHR on Tuesday, Thursday, Saturday, and Sunday.

Monday: Run 10 minutes at 70 percent MHR; run 5 minutes at 80 to 85 percent MHR with elevation; run 5 minutes at 70 percent MHR.

Wednesday: Run 5 minutes at 70 percent MHR; run 3 minutes at 80 to 85 percent MHR; jog 1 minute; run 3 minutes at 80 to 85 percent MHR; run 5 minutes at 70 percent MHR.

Friday: Run 5 minutes at 70 percent MHR; run 4 minutes at 80 to 85 percent MHR; jog slowly 1 minute; run 2 minutes at 80 to 85 percent MHR; run 8 minutes at 70 percent MHR.

Week 7: Run 20 to 30 minutes at 70 percent MHR on Tuesday, Thursday, Saturday, and Sunday.

Monday: Run 10 minutes at 70 percent MHR; run 5 minutes, at an elevation, at 80 to 85 percent MHR; run 14 minutes at 70 percent MHR.

Wednesday: Run 5 minutes at 70 percent MHR; run 2 minutes at 80 to 85 percent MHR; jog 1 minute; run 2 minutes at 80 to 85 percent MHR; run 5 minutes at 70 percent MHR.

Friday: Run 50 minutes at 70 percent MHR.

Medical Problems

Injuries from treadmill use will basically come from overuse problems or from strain. Following are the four most common injuries you may suffer in the course of your treadmill workouts and what you can do to treat them yourself.

ACHILLES TENDONITIS

The Achilles tendon runs from the back of the heel bone to the calf muscles. It allows you to walk, jump, and run. By exercising and using your calf muscles, or simply by pounding out the mileage on your treadmill, you may cause the Achilles tendon to become inflamed. Actually, what has happened is that the tendon has developed tiny tears, and this causes it to swell and throb.

Achilles tendonitis will generally develop from many hard workouts on the treadmill combined with wearing poorly designed or worn-out running shoes. You will feel a dull, aching pain in the area of the Achilles tendon just above the back of your running shoe. Exercising—going for a run—actually seems to make the pain go away, or at least subside. For this reason, many exercisers don't know enough to stop running. They think that since their tendon no longer hurts as they run, the injury

Stretching my Achilles tendons with a wall push-up.

is getting better. Actually, it's only getting worse. Once you have cooled down, the pain comes on even stronger. Continuing to run without any form of treatment will aggravate the condition and in extreme cases can eventually lead to a rupture of the tendon.

If you have tendonitis, treatment should be started at once. *Stop running.* This does not mean stop exercising! If you have access, you can still swim, bike, or row with virtually no ill effects to the tendon. Ice the tendon twice daily and take aspirin to reduce the inflammation. When you are finally pain free—and this could be 7 to 14 days later—begin wall push-up stretching exercises (see below). Stretching is the only effective preventive measure that you can take. From now on, stretch each time before you run, or else you will risk a recurrence of your injury.

You can resume your treadmill program with drastically reduced mileage once you are pain free. It may be better to start with a fast walking program on the treadmill. Increase speed gradually and see how the tendon feels. Refrain from using the elevation setting on the treadmill. Running uphill puts too much strain on the Achilles tendon.

Many times Achilles tendonitis is brought on or at least aggravated by poor equipment. If your running shoes are worn down at the heels, have them repaired or buy a new pair. Wearing orthotics or shoe wedges may offer some relief by supporting the tendons.

How to do a Wall Push-Up

Perhaps the best pre-exercise stretch you can do is the wall push-up. This simple stretch will gently tug and stretch the Achilles tendon out to its normal length.

1. Stand back at arm's length from the wall.
2. With your back straight and heels on the floor, place your palms on the wall.
3. Bend your elbows as you would in a regular push-up and let your body move closer to the wall. Hold here for the count of 10. Do 10 or more reps.

CHONDROMALACIA

Knee problems will strike one out of four runners during their active careers. Treadmill runners are just as vulnerable. The most common of all knee ailments is chondromalacia, often called "runner's knee." Chondromalacia is a very painful condition brought on by excessive pronation, a tilting inward of the ankles as you run. This causes the back of the kneecap to rub against the thigh bone, which then starts to soften the kneecap.

Telltale signs of chondromalacia include the following:

- stiffness in the knee
- occasional locking of the knee as you walk or run
- pain whenever you bend your knee
- a grinding noise in the knee area when you bend the knee

If your problem is biomechanical and you have either a leg-length discrepancy or pronating feet, consult your chiropractor, orthopedist, or podiatrist. He or she may recommend arch supports or orthotic devices to relieve your condition. These devices will prevent your ankles from tilting inward as well as keep your ankles, knees, and pelvis in alignment.

If you have chondromalacia, home treatment that you can start yourself includes rest, ice, compression, and elevation (see RICE, p. 215) for the first few days. Once the pain has subsided, you can begin a weight-training program to build up the quadriceps of the front thigh. These muscles, which get very little use while running, will add stability to the kneecap once they are properly strengthened.

Chondromalacia comes and goes depending on your exercise intensity and the preventive measures you take. When the strength of both legs seems to be equal and the pain in the knee has disappeared, start your workouts on the treadmill, but at a reduced level. Be sure to ice the injured knee(s) for 10 to 15 minutes after each workout. Before going to bed, use moist heat on the knee. Continue with all these measures until you are sure the problem is cured.

If you still have pain after all these measures, consult your physician. In rare cases, surgery may be necessary.

PLANTAR FASCIITIS

The plantar fascia is a ligament on the sole of the foot that runs from the heel bone to each of your five toes. It serves as the main support for the bottom of the foot. Plantar fasciitis is a tear of this tendon and is caused by wearing poorly padded running shoes or by suffering a sharp blow to the bottom of the foot. Remember, every time your foot comes down on the treadmill belt, three to five times your body weight is absorbed by your foot. Too much pounding and something will surely give. Often, it's your plantar fascia.

Signs of plantar fasciitis include a dull, throbbing pain on the sole of your foot, especially pronounced near the heel. The pain is quite notice-able when you awaken and continues to throb as you walk around during the day. If you try running, the pain flares up immediately.

Many runners and exercise fanatics can't bear to read this, but if you have plantar fasciitis it will take a long time to heal. To aid the healing process, ice the area for 10 to 15 minutes twice daily. Put full-size arch supports or orthotics into your street and running shoes. This seems to help many people. But if these measures don't bring any relief after a few weeks, contact your physician. You may need medical attention.

SHIN SPLINTS

Overuse and/or muscle imbalance are the main causes of shin splints. This makes the lining of the tibia (the bone located on the front inside of the leg) throb and swell anywhere along its length from the ankle to just below the knee. In severe cases the pain is so intense that it may feel as if someone has hit your shin with a hammer. Once you stop running, the pain goes away. But if you start running again without proper treatment, the pain will return immediately.

Wall push-ups and RICE may bring some relief. Another good way to rehabilitate yourself once the pain has decreased is to walk up flights of stairs. This will add strength to the shin muscle, a muscle that has grown weak solely because of the overdevelopment of the calf muscle from running. By strengthening the muscles that you usually stretch in running (shin), and by stretching the muscles that you usually strengthen in running (calf), you will eventually clear up the problem of shin splints by bringing about balance to your agonist and antagonist muscles.

Orthotics

In the past decade, runners have made orthotics almost as popular as running shoes. Orthotics are actually custom-fit leather or molded plastic shoe inserts made from casts of your feet. Used with athletic footwear, orthotics will correct most biomechanical imbalances that affect your posture and therefore can cause knee and back problems.

What orthotics do for someone with a foot imbalance is to place the foot in a neutral position. As you begin to run on the treadmill, the orthotic will correct any leg-length discrepancy or ankle-pronation problem simply by keeping the foot in balance, preventing it from tipping inward or outward.

Orthotics aren't for everyone. According to some orthopedists, they aren't for anyone. But if you have a recurring foot, knee, or back problem that doesn't get better and you want to do something about it, orthotics might be the answer.

Before going to a podiatrist or chiropractor for orthotics, try a pair of over-the-counter inserts available in pharmacies or sporting-goods stores. If these don't help you, consult your podiatrist or chiropractor. A good pair of orthotics starts at about $75.

Select Equipment

NONMOTORIZED TREADMILLS

Landice Products Corporation
269 East Blackwell St.
Dover, NJ 07801
(201) 328-6560

LANDICE FITNESS MILL

Length: 57¼"
Width: 24¼"
Weight: 60 lbs.
Elevation: up to a 17¼% grade
Speed: Slow walk to 8 mph
Cost: $785

The Fitness Mill is a superb nonmotorized treadmill that has a patented speed-control system that regulates speed as accurately as a motorized unit. An easy-to-reach knob on the front console sets the speed. The front panel also has a digital timer and speedometer. Elevation is adjusted by hand.

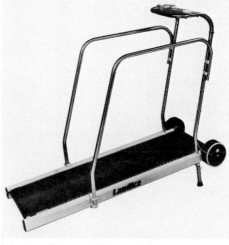
Landice Fitness Mill

Sportech, Inc.
PO Box 99101
Cleveland, OH 44119
(800) 221-1258

SPORTECH AEROBIC TRAINER

Length: 6'
Width: 26"
Weight: 250 lbs.
Elevation: from 3% to 13%
Speed: Up to 12 mph
Cost: $1,195

Sportech has a high-quality nonmotorized treadmill that offers the competitive runner a great indoor training alternative. It's possible to do hill work, distance running, sprints, and intervals on the Aerobic Trainer. The elevation settings go up to 13 percent. Try the settings: 1 mile run at 7 percent is equal in effort to 2.5 miles on a flat surface.

Sportech Aerobic Trainer

MOTORIZED TREADMILLS

Landice Products Corporation
269 East Blackwell St.
Dover, NJ 07801
(201) 328-6560

LANDICE POWER MILL II

Length: 63"
Width: 24.5"
Weight: 125 lbs.
Elevation: none
Speed: 0–9 mph
Cost: $1,375

Walk, jog, or run on the Power Mill II, a treadmill designed for years of dependable home training. Speed changes are made simply by turning the waist-high control knob in front of you. The front panel also includes a digital timer to measure workout time.

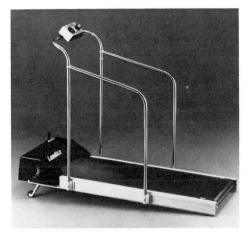
Landice Power Mill II

Ogden Health Products
PO Box 148
Schererville, IN 46375
(219) 322-5252

TM PACER

Length: 63.5″
Width: 32″
Weight: 90 lbs.
Elevation: 0–27%
Speed: 2–3.5 mph
Cost: $550

For anyone interested in a walking program, here's a basic motorized treadmill with elevation that can't be beat for price or quality. Speed on the TM Pacer is changed quickly and easily: shut off the motor, lift up the plastic hood, and switch the drive belt.

Precor USA
PO Box 1018
Redmond, WA 98073
(800) 662-0606

PRECOR 910ei TREADMILL

Length: 72″
Width: 26″
Weight: 155 lbs.
Elevation: 0–15% grade
Speed: 1–8 mph
Cost: $2,295

An easy-to-reach fingertip pad gets you started walking on this high-tech treadmill from Precor. Digital display gives your total elapsed time, speed, and mileage. The gas-assisted arm in front of the treadmill raises the unit easily from flat to a 15 percent grade, giving you great diversity in your workouts.

PRECOR 935e TREADMILL

Length: 75″
Width: 28¼″
Weight: 165 lbs.
Speed: 1–10 mph
Cost: $2,695

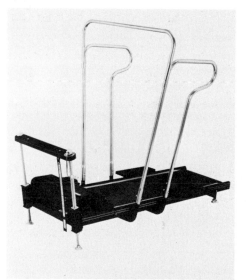

TM Pacer

Precor 910ei Treadmill

This Precor treadmill is a beauty. Incredibly smooth to run on, it goes up to 10 mph at the touch of the key pad. With its powerful microprocessor it also calculates your caloric expenditure, time, speed, and total distance.

Universal
PO Box 1270
Cedar Rapids, IA 52406
(800) 553-7901

TREDEX 2924

Length: 81″
Width: 25″
Weight: 230 lbs.
Speed: 1–8 mph
Cost: $2,500

Plug in the Tredex from Universal and you're all set to walk, jog, or run in the comfort of your own home. The computerized control panel shows speed, running time, distance and pace per mile in an easy-to-read, digital display. On–off, pause, reset, and speed controls all operate with a touch of your finger.

Trotter Treadmills, Inc.
24 Hopedale St.
Hopedale, MA 01747
(800) 227-1632

PRITIKIN PROMISE

Length: 61″
Width: 24″
Weight: 225 lbs.
Elevation: 1.8–15%
Speed: 2.2–9.2 mph
Cost: $2,995

Here's the treadmill chosen by the Pritikin Centers to be used in their health centers around the country. The Pritikin Promise offers an ultraquiet AC-drive motor, automatic elevation at the press of the key pad, and an easy-to-read digital display showing distance, speed, and pace.

Precor 935e Treadmill

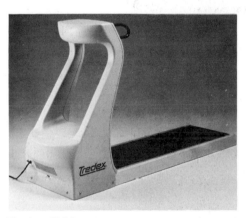
Tredex 2924

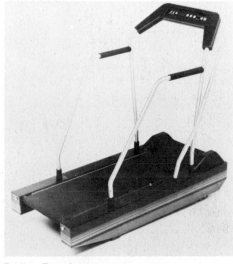
Pritikin Promise

EIGHT

CROSS-COUNTRY SKIING

Why Ski?

Cross-country, or Nordic, skiing is at the top of the list when it comes to offering the most beneficial aerobic exercise. Physicians, physical therapists, exercise physiologists, and athletes alike rank it as superior to all other types of aerobic workouts available because it exercises every muscle in the body from your shoulders to your toes. The basic reason for this is that cross-country skiing involves both leg and arm movements, working simultaneously in smooth and rhythmic kicks, glides, and poling motions.

To be really fit you need an exercise program that will add to your flexibility, strength, and cardiovascular endurance. Using a cross-country ski machine at home will certainly give you all of these things. "A cross-country ski machine will provide you all of this because it utilizes both the arms and legs together," says Doug Allen, a researcher at the

167

Oregon State University's exercise lab who is also directing a study to determine which aerobic home-exercise equipment actually gives the best workout. "A cross-country ski machine gives a total-body workout," says Allen. "You use your arms and upper body for 'poling,' and your lower body for propulsion when you move your legs back and forth. The best thing about the workout is that you can get your heart rate up to your target zone very quickly, but your body is worked gently. When you're finished exercising, you're tired, but because you've been sliding back and forth, as opposed to lifting and then dropping your feet down as you do in running, you don't ache at all."

Norm Oakvik, a Minnesotan who competed in the 1956 winter Olympic Games in the Nordic combined, a grueling two-part event consisting of a 15-kilometer cross-country ski race followed by a ski-jump competition, uses his NordicTrack cross-country ski machine daily. Oakvik, now in his mid-fifties, has a chronic sore back and a damaged hip, the result of a car accident several years ago. But on many days he still skis on the ski machine in his home for more than an hour. "The cross-country ski movement is so smooth that it doesn't hurt my back or my hip," claims Oakvik. "I get a great aerobic workout every time out."

Oakvik, who also coaches a junior boys' cross-country ski team, sees the cross-country ski machine as an important training tool for his team's preseason workouts, not only because of its great conditioning aspects but because a good machine can duplicate the actual cross-country ski movement so closely. "Of course, you can't double-pole or skate on the machine like you can outdoors on skis, but because you're using the same muscles on a machine as you do when you ski outdoors, I'd say that a cross-country ski machine is a darn good piece of equipment to use if you're interested in staying in shape."

"The NordicTrack cross-country ski machine is perfect for rehabilitation programs," claims Dr. Fred Nelson, a Bethesda, Maryland, orthopedist who makes great use of the ski machine with many of his patients. "I have many patients with ankle, knee, hip, or back problems who just can't exercise on any conventional home machine because of their physical condition. But with the cross-country ski machine there's no problem at all because there's virtually no stress or strain on the joints. A person is able to work both upper and lower muscle groups at the same time."

A 3:18 marathon runner, Dr. Nelson also incorporates home skiing as part of his own personal running program. When it's too icy or cold to run outdoors, or when he's injured himself from running, he'll go for an indoor ski workout instead. "It's a great piece," says Dr. Nelson. "I can easily duplicate my seven-minute-mile running pace on the machine and this way still keep up with my running training."

Using a cross-country ski machine has been called the perfect exercise because the basic movement demands that the feet glide smoothly into position to support the body rather than brought down vertically as in running. This horizontal kicking back and gliding forward movement eliminates almost all shock and pounding to the body. Because of this, injuries from home cross-country ski programs are almost nonexistent; the exerciser gets all the benefits of a running workout without any of the bad effects to the musculoskeletal system that you can get from running.

It takes as little as two minutes to learn how to ski on the NordicTrack. Beginners and those with back problems can start out by holding on to the front bumper pad.

The NordicTrack cross-country ski machine is the first piece of equipment that out-of-condition people are started out on at the H.E.A.R. Institute, an exercise and physical rehabilitation facility in Red Bank, New Jersey. "The ski machine is relatively simple to learn how to use," says Phil Dunphy, director of the institute. "It takes as little as two minutes to learn how to ski on the machine, even for the nonathletic types." Dunphy starts all beginners without using the ski poles. They either hold on to the front bumper pad or keep their arms comfortably at their sides. This way they remain as upright as possible as they exercise.

The importance of keeping this upright position during exercise is one of the principal reasons why Phil Dunphy is so keen on the NordicTrack cross-country ski machine and why he recommends it to anyone who asks which piece of home exercise equipment to buy.

"Your typical American sits all day slumped over at his or her desk, talking on the phone, writing, or staring into a computer terminal," says Dunphy. "Gravity is bending them, pulling, curling them over, and making them slump.

"This resulting bad posture stretches their back muscles and this eventually leads to all the back problems that we're seeing today in almost epidemic proportions. Also, the more technological and less physical our society becomes, the more these back problems will worsen."

The best solution to all this disheartening news, says Dunphy, is to choose a home exercise that will reverse what gravity and your sedentary job are doing to you. Dunphy strongly recommends exercise that is first of all aerobic; you need to condition your heart and your lungs. The exercise should also keep you in a good postural position and burn a lot of calories as you perform it.

Home exercises that meet Dunphy's criteria include walking, running, or riding a stationary bicycle sitting straight up without holding on to the handlebars. Or else you can use a NordicTrack cross-country ski machine in your home. "When people get on a ski machine they're forced to stand up straight and stretch their back muscles," says Dunphy. "What they are doing—and this makes the exercise so good—is that they're reversing a position that they've more than likely been in all day. They're now fully extending their bodies, maintaining and using it the way the body was supposed to be used in the first place."

The NordicTrack is also an excellent exerciser for anyone with lower-back problems. "Adjust the bumper pad so it will be against the pelvis and then hold on to the sides of the pad," says Dr. Nelson. "This way, as you ski, you'll block the rotation of the pelvis, thereby preventing any torque from being applied to your back." Skiing like this, says Dr.

Nelson, effectively exercises your hamstrings, calves, and gluteal muscles. The muscles are worked hard but in a very normal vertical position, so there is little strain.

What to Look For in a Ski Machine

Components

The NordicTrack is the only ski machine I've used that is solidly constructed, easy to operate, and gives a consistently high-quality workout. The others that I've tried can't compare, and for this reason the NordicTrack is the only one described here.

The NordicTrack was invented in 1976 by Ed Pauls, a Chaska, Minnesota, mechanical engineer who was desperately seeking a suitable way to train for cross-country skiing, his weekend exercise passion. Job constraints, lack of snow, and freezing temperatures often made it difficult for Pauls to exercise with any consistency, so he set out to invent a machine that could duplicate the ski motions particular to cross-country and also be portable and compact enough to be used indoors. After a year of work, trial and error, the first NordicTrack prototype was tested and marketed to cross-country skiers. The initial popular reception among skiers in and around Minnesota led to slow but steady word-of-mouth advertising and referrals. In the ensuing years, avid skiers and exercise enthusiasts helped skyrocket annual sales of the NordicTrack to eighteen thousand. Ed's daughter, Terri, helped prove the NordicTrack's effectiveness by training on it and subsequently winning the National Collegiate Cross-country Ski Championship in March 1985.

The NordicTrack Pro model is a rugged oak unit that weighs 63 pounds and needs only a 2-by-7-foot space in order to be set up for a workout. It's sold only by mail order from PSI, 124 Columbia Court, Chaska, MN 55318 (800) 328-5888. The Pro model costs $560 plus shipping. A lighter weight version (model 505) costs $470.

If lack of sufficient space is a problem for you and you can't keep the unit permanently in one spot, the NordicTrack can easily be folded up in seconds to a tidy 18-by-23-by-45-inch bundle and wheeled away to be stored vertically in a closet.

If you're an apartment dweller, downstairs neighbors may be somewhat of a problem if the vibrations from the machine are allowed to travel through the floor as you ski. Put a plywood board or a thick rug under the machine. Dan Levin, a *Sports Illustrated* magazine writer and home-exercise devotee, simply wheels his NordicTrack out onto his apartment balcony overlooking the East River in Manhattan whenever he wants to go for an hour-long ski session. "This way I keep the guy downstairs from pounding on his living-room ceiling and yelling up at me," says Levin. "I'm not disturbing him, and he's not disturbing my workout."

Form and Technique

The cross-country skiing movement consists of two parts, the kick and the glide. Once you master these lower-body movements and then combine them with the upper-body poling technique, your exercise sessions will be rhythmical and pleasant, and as uncomplicated and natural as walking.

THE KICK

To begin, set the arm resistance tension and leg resistance tension to the lowest settings. However, if at this time you don't feel coordinated enough, don't use the poles. Instead, as you ski, just keep your arms at your sides and move them as you would when you walk.

To start skiing, push the front of your training shoes into the rubber toe pieces at the front of the skis. These ski "bindings" will keep your feet positioned on the sliding oak skis. Adjust the bumper pad so that the lower portion of it is parallel to your pelvis, just low enough that when your leg comes forward the pad doesn't interfere with your thigh. The purpose of the pad is to keep you from moving forward off the front of the track.

Next place all your weight flat on one ski and kick (push) it to the rear. This will start the rollers that drive the flywheel through the one-way clutch device. Slide the foot back as far as it will comfortably go. Your heel should be lifted off the ski at the end of the kick.

THE GLIDE

Now, glide the foot back toward the front of the machine. Keep your weight off this foot till it is directly under your body. Then put all your

The rhythmical kick and glide movement of cross-country skiing puts little stress on your skeletal system.

weight evenly back on the foot. Note that this is not a shuffling motion. The weight is shifted alternately from one foot to the other just as in running. If you are using the "ski poles," pull the arms opposite your kicking foot back past your hips. Use long pole strokes to gain the most muscle involvement. If not poling, just move your arms in a normal walking or running motion.

Home Ski Tips

The following tips will make your home ski workouts much more enjoyable.

1.   Since you are using both your upper and lower body as you ski, you will perspire rather freely. Keep a towel handy to wipe your arms and face. Exercise in a well-ventilated room. If it gets too warm, use an electric fan aimed up at your legs and chest.

2.   Keep a water bottle handy and drink every 5 minutes or less as you ski. Keeping well hydrated as you exercise is a key ingredient to any successful workout.

3.   If you are a serious cross-country skier, use an old pair of skis and bindings on the NordicTrack. Simply remove the standard-issue oak skis and replace them with your own. Cut down the tips of the skis so that they'll fit under the front bar of the machine. Cutting the tips will not ruin the skis for outdoor use; they can still be used with no loss in performance, in most instances. This gives you the added advantage of being able to break in a new pair of ski boots before the ski season begins.

4.   Listen to music as you ski. Selecting your favorite music will make the workout seem to go much faster as well as get you motivated.

5.   For advanced skiers, you can easily lessen the pressure you feel on the bumper pad at higher resistance levels by placing the front end of the NordicTrack atop several books or a cinderblock. Set resistance levels accordingly. As you ski, your pelvis should just be touching the front pad.

6.   If you are a racer and are using the NordicTrack as an adjunct to your outdoor ski training, you will find that the NordicTrack accurately duplicates the motion used in going up hills. One thing that it won't give you, however, is trail savvy. Get out and practice outdoors whenever possible.

7.   Cross-country skiing is a total-body conditioner. According to Bill Koch, of Eugene, Oregon, silver medalist in the 30-kilometer cross-country ski race in the 1976 winter Olympics and 1982 World Cup champion, working out twice a week on the NordicTrack will slowly increase your fitness level. You won't improve as fast as someone who exercises three times a week, but your fitness will improve. Skiing four to five times a week is probably optimal. If you ski more than that, says Koch, you're skiing for something besides fitness.

Ski Workouts

"The biggest mistake beginners make with the NordicTrack," says Bill Koch, "is that they start off too intensely, not realizing how much more their cardiovascular system is worked when arms and legs are worked in unison in the cross-country ski motion. So they hop on, set both the arm and leg tension too high, and within two minutes they've completely exhausted themselves."

The problem that then unfolds is that home exercisers start to notice the creeping shadow of failure coming into their workout room. They start to believe that they just don't have what it takes to use the machine. And this isn't at all true. "To have a successful exercise

World champion Bill Koch working out on a NordicTrack.

program using a NordicTrack," says Koch, "you have to start easy and move up slowly in your workouts, increasing both the duration and intensity levels in small increments."

Aerobic conditioning takes time. Depending on your current conditioning level, building an adequate aerobic base can take as long as two months of 20-to-45-minute workouts three times a week. But whatever your exercise level may be, remember that training is your own personal adventure. Don't try to rush it or compare your work with that of a friend. You'll only set back your workouts and curtail your progress.

BEGINNER

Beginners are those exercisers who have a hard time walking up a flight of stairs without breathing hard or feeling pain in the leg muscles. If this sounds like you, the following workout is geared at your level. You are untrained aerobically and your goal is to start building the foundation of an aerobic base.

Total time: 5 minutes, every day
Target heart rate: 55–60 percent of maximum heart rate

Set resistance to the lowest setting. Don't use the handgrips or hold on to the pad. Simply keep your arms at your sides and use your legs. Kick and glide back and forth for 5 minutes. Get off the machine when the allotted time is up. You're finished. If you have the opportunity, do this exercise several times during the day.

Over a period of time, start to build on your beginning workouts, increasing the tension setting slightly and adding 1 minute to the workout when you feel that you're ready for it. Once you feel that you have no trouble with balance, begin to use the ski poles. Keep the tension setting low. When you are up to 20 to 30 minutes of nonstop skiing, you're ready for the next level.

INTERMEDIATE

If you can ski nonstop at 5 mph for 20 to 45 minutes, you are ready to begin intermediate-level workouts.

Bill Koch, one of the top cross-country skiers in the world, offers a choice of three types of home workouts on the NordicTrack. The first type of workout he calls "endurance," which is an LSD routine. The

CROSS-COUNTRY SKIING   177

second type is a bit more demanding; Koch calls these three-tiered routines "constants." In these workouts you have to raise your speed and resistance level and hold it "constant" for more than 10 minutes before slowing down. Koch's third type of workout is an interval; like the constants, it has three different levels for you to try.

WORKOUT 1

ENDURANCE

Total time: 30–60 minutes, up to three times a week
Target heart rate: 70–75 percent of maximum heart rate

5–10 minutes: Ski at low resistance and speed, adjusting tension so you get a comfortable level that can be continued for the rest of the workout.
20–40 minutes: Ski at this tension level at 6 to 12 mph, maintaining your target heart rate for at least 20 uninterrupted minutes.
5–10 minutes: Cool down by skiing with less tension and speed.

WORKOUT 2

CONSTANT (short)

Total time: 25–45 minutes, not more than three times a week
Target heart rate: 75–80 percent of maximum heart rate

5–10 minutes: Warm up with easy skiing, gradually increasing tension and speed.
15–25 minutes: Ski at 8 to 16 mph and hold it at this level for 2 to 3 minutes. You should be skiing within your target heart zone at this point, though you may go out of the zone at the end of each stint if this feels comfortable. Take a short rest period after the constant is finished by skiing easy for up to 2 minutes. Don't let your heart rate drop more than 35 beats. When the recovery time is over, start skiing at speed once again for another 2 to 3 minutes. Repeat this constant and recovery workout as many times as you can. Resistance levels should not be so high as to push you into anaerobic exercise.
5–10 minutes: Easy skiing to cool down.

WORKOUT 3

CONSTANT (Medium)

Total time: 25–45 minutes
Target heart rate: 75–80 percent of maximum heart rate

5–10 minutes: Warm up.
15–25 minutes: Ski for 3 to 5 minutes at speeds between 8 and 16 mph. Take 2 to 3 minutes of easy skiing for recovery between your next constant. Repeat as much as you like.
5–10 minutes: Cool down with easy skiing.

WORKOUT 4

CONSTANT (Long)

Total time: 25–45 minutes
Target heart rate: 75–80 percent of maximum heart rate

5–10 minutes: Warm up.
15–25 minutes: Go hard at speeds between 8 and 16 mph and hold it at this level for 5 to 10 minutes. Recovery consists of easy skiing for 3 to 4 minutes before beginning the next constant.
5–10 minutes: Cool down with easy skiing.

WORKOUT 5

INTERVALS (Power)

Total time: 30–45 minutes, not more than three times a week
Target heart rate: 80–90 percent of maximum heart rate

5–10 minutes: Warm up with easy skiing.
20–25 minutes: After establishing a good resistance level in your warm-up, sprint out at maximum power and speed for 20 to 25 seconds. The speedometer should register 10 to 20 mph. Recovery time between sprints is up to 75 seconds. Adjust length, recovery time, and speed during the workout to stay within your target zone. Repeat intervals as often as you like during the workout. Be cautious about doing this workout two days in a row. It may be too taxing for your body.
5–10 minutes: Cool down with easy skiing.

WORKOUT 6

INTERVAL (Medium)

Total time: 35–45 minutes, not more than three times a week
Target heart rate: 80–90 percent of maximum heart rate

5–10 minutes: Warm up.
20–25 minutes: Ski hard at near maximum power and speed for 30–60 seconds. Speedometer should register 10 20 mph or more. The recovery period between sprints is up to 90 seconds. Repeat.
5–10 minutes: Cool down with easy skiing.

WORKOUT 7

INTERVALS (Long)

Total time: 30–40 minutes, not more than three times a week
Target heart rate: 80–90 percent of maximum heart rate

5–10 minutes: Warm up.
15–25 minutes: Ski hard for 60–120 seconds. Speedometer should register between 10 and 20 mph. Recovery period is 75 seconds or more. Repeat.
5–10 minutes: Cool down.

ADVANCED

In order to reach this level you should be able to complete intermediate workouts with no problem. Do not attempt these advanced workouts if you still have trouble at the intermediate level.

WORKOUT 1

ENDURANCE

Total time: 45 minutes or longer
Target heart rate: 75–85 percent of maximum heart rate

5–15 minutes: Warm up slowly, establishing proper leg and arm resistance settings.
40 minutes or longer: Skiing at 8 to 16 mph, continue at your target heart rate pace for as long as you wish. You should not feel tired during the

first thirty minutes. If you do, the tension levels are too high and should be adjusted accordingly. Don't ski to exhaustion.
5–10 minutes: Cool down at low resistance.

WORKOUT 2

CONSTANT (Short)

Total time: 30–40 minutes
Target heart rate: 80–90 percent of maximum heart rate

5–10 minutes: Warm up slowly to increase your heart rate.
20 minutes or more: Ski hard at 12 to 20 mph and hold it at this speed for 3–5 minutes. Recovery time is up to 2 minutes. Don't let heart rate drop more than 25 beats from your target heart rate. Repeat.
5–10 minutes: Cool down with easy skiing.

WORKOUT 3

CONSTANT (Medium)

Total time: 30–40 minutes
Target heart rate: 80–90 percent of maximum heart rate

5–10 minutes: Warm up gradually to raise your heart rate to your range.
20 minutes or longer: Sprint out and hold speed between 12 and 20 mph for 5–10 minutes. Recovery periods between each constant should be 2–3 minutes. Repeat.
5–10 minutes: Cool down with easy skiing.

WORKOUT 4

CONSTANT (Long)

Total time: 30–60 minutes
Target heart rate: 80–90 percent of maximum heart rate

5–10 minutes: Warm up with easy skiing, steadily increasing speed.
20 minutes or longer: Sprint out and hold speed between 12 and 20 mph for 10–15 minutes. Recovery period is up to 4 minutes between constants. Repeat.
5–10 minutes: Cool down with easy skiing.

WORKOUT 5

INTERVALS (Power)

Total time: 30–40 minutes
Target heart rate: 85–95 (or higher) percent of maximum heart rate

5–10 minutes: Warm up with easy skiing to set proper resistance settings.
20 minutes or longer: Sprint out and hold speed for 30–45 seconds at speeds of 15–25 mph or higher. Recovery period is up to 75 seconds. Repeat.
5–10 minutes: Cool down with easy skiing.

WORKOUT 6

INTERVALS (Medium)

Total time: 30–40 minutes
Target heart rate: 85–95 (or higher) percent of maximum heart rate

5–10 minutes: Warm up with easy skiing, gradually increasing speed and power.
20 minutes or longer: Ski very hard and hold for 45–75 seconds at 15–25 mph. Recovery time is up to 90 seconds. Repeat.
5–10 minutes: Cool down.

WORKOUT 7

INTERVALS (Long)

Total time: 30–40 minutes
Target heart rate: 85–95 (or higher) percent of maximum heart rate

5–10 minutes: Warm up.
20 minutes or longer: Ski very hard 75–150 seconds at 15–25 mph. Recovery is for 75 or more seconds. Repeat.
5–10 minutes: Cool down with easy skiing.

HEART-RATE
MONITORS

FOR ANY HOME EXERCISE PROGRAM TO BE SUCCESSFUL, IT HAS TO be enjoyable. You have to like what you're doing or else those half-hour sessions three to seven times a week will dwindle down to nothing. But, more important, to be successful, your home exercise routine has to be a safe one. Taking your pulse regularly as you exercise is the first step to ensure that you aren't overstressing your heart. When you are running on a treadmill, rowing, skiing, or cycling at home, taking your pulse is the best way to ensure that you are getting maximum health benefits by exercising hard enough to give your heart a workout. By determining your target heart rate (see p. 24) and exercising within the borders of these medically approved heartbeat ranges for a minimum of 20 uninterrupted minutes, exercise physiologists say you will achieve substantial aerobic benefits. A simple pulse check will tell you if you are working within these limits.

According to medical authorities, exercise that falls below your target heart zone doesn't work the heart enough and therefore is not as beneficial as most people think. On the other hand, going too hard and surpassing your target heart zone may overstress the heart and be dangerous to your health. Checking your pulse as you exercise will end these problems.

There are two ways of taking your pulse. Most people will pause during exercise and place three middle fingers over the radial artery of the wrist, count the beats for 6 seconds, and multiply the result by 10 to get their current pulse. By knowing their target heart zone, they can then keep exercising at the same pace, or increase or decrease intensity accordingly.

Taking your pulse by hand is certainly cheaper than investing money in an electronic heart-rate monitor, but it's not the best way to take your

Taking your pulse by hand.

pulse. There are three major drawbacks to taking your pulse by hand as you exercise:

1.   Most people don't know how to take their pulse or are just unable to locate their pulse.

2.   Once you stop exercising in order to take your pulse, your pulse starts to drop rapidly. To get an accurate pulse reading just after an exercise bout requires that you catch your breath, quickly locate your pulse, and then start counting. Often people aren't quick enough to do this and therefore don't get an accurate reading.

The target heart zone recommended by the American Heart Association is only 20 beats wide, high and low. If you take your pulse by hand and have even as little as a 5 percent error, you can go too high or low from your target zone in your workout.

3. Taking your pulse interrupts the flow of your workout and may give you an excuse to eventually stop taking your pulse or else quit the workout earlier than planned.

Electronic Tikker Trackers

Electronic alternatives to taking your pulse by hand are now available. Heart-rate monitors (or pulse meters, as they're more commonly called) are excellent devices for giving you a constant pulse readout as you exercise. No longer do you have to stop and take your pulse. Simply by glancing down at the small watchband or the playing-card-sized monitor strapped to your waist or exercise machine, you can get a digital readout of your heart's work and continue exercising without missing a stride or stroke.

Having a pulse meter is like having a speedometer on a car. It takes the guesswork out of determining your current pulse and tells you exactly how fast your heart is beating. Most people are surprised to find that when they first start to train with a pulse meter they don't have to train as hard as they used to. This is because in many cases, prior to using a heart-rate monitor these people had actually been training at the higher ranges of their target heart zone and didn't even know it. Their exercise was not only especially hard but potentially dangerous because they may have been overstressing their hearts. Now, by using a pulse monitor, these "overexercisers" can cut back on their exercise intensity and therefore have a safer and much more enjoyable time by exercising with less strain and effort.

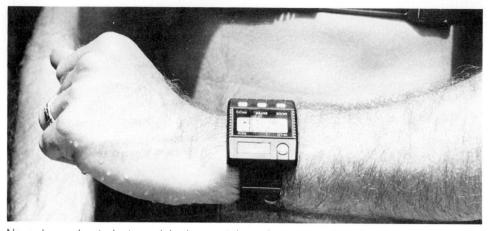

Never lose a beat. Just a quick glance at the pulsemeter as I work out and I know for certain just how hard I'm really going.

Currently there are almost three dozen heart-rate monitors available, most of them made by one Japanese manufacturer and marketed under different names in this country. Unfortunately, most of these heart-rate monitors are unreliable or inaccurate. However, there are some good-quality monitors available. Some give you not only your pulse reading as you exercise but have added features such as beepers that alert you when you are either below or above your target heart zone. One state-of-the-art monitor, the Benchmark Quantum XL Fitness Monitor from AMF, has programmable functions to record your pulse every 5 or 15 seconds throughout your workout. It can then give the heart-rate information back to you when you're finished. You can either plot your heart rate by hand on a graph or hook up the wristwatch unit to a computer to get instant and detailed feedback about your heart during every phase of your workout.

Although the monitors that combine the best of the electronic world can cost almost double the base price of a simple yet high-quality heart-rate monitor, the additional feedback you get from these gadgets makes the expense worthwhile. All information about your heart during the workout can be recorded and you can begin to accurately program your weekly exercise based on how your heart responds to it.

At present there are two distinct types of pulse meters available. The photo-optical pulse monitor is adequate for rowing, skiing, and cycling programs. To use this type of heart-rate monitor, you simply clip a sensor to your ear lobe and attach the base unit and connecting wires to your exercise machine. The unit registers pulse by shooting a light beam into the capillaries of your ear lobes, counting your pulse by registering the systolic beat of your blood flow. The maximum heart rate that these units can register is generally 170 bpm. However, for treadmill running, the constant movement associated with running and the interference created by the metal plates of a treadmill are enough to render these pulse meters inaccurate. If you are involved in a treadmill program, you'll have to purchase the heart-rate monitor that uses a chest strap and electrodes.

To use a chest-strap monitor you attach a strap or belt containing electrodes around your chest just below your breast bone. Heart rate is recorded by the electrodes on the chest strap, which read the heart's signals and relay them—depending on the system—via two wires, radio waves, or your own body, to a wrist unit or playing card-sized monitor where the pulse is displayed digitally on a liquid crystal screen.

The better heart-rate monitors use a chest strap and are perfect for all home workout machinery. Although some people may complain that these units are a bit confining, their accuracy is astounding. But, as with the photo-optical monitor, there are some minor problems with these chest-strap monitors. Too much chest hair, profuse sweating, or too much body fat can cause some of the monitors to give inaccurate readings. Also, being born with too faint a pulse will render the unit useless, because it won't be able to accurately detect the pulse.

I strongly recommend that if you are going to spend $160 to $300 for a pulse meter, you go to your sporting-goods store dressed in your workout clothes. Hook up a pulse meter that you like to a machine that you use at home and exercise for 15 minutes. This test will not only acquaint you with the workings of the pulse unit but, more important, assure you that it can work for you.

Select Equipment

If you really want to be serious about your home exercise program, a heart-rate monitor is the next best thing to actually having a coach in the room with you to make sure you get the most out of your workout. The monitor peers into your body and lets you know instantly just how your heart, the true indicator of exercise intensity, is doing.

The following units represent the best heart-rate monitors on the market today.

AMF American
200 American Way
Jefferson, IA 50129
(800) 247-3978

BENCHMARK QUANTUM XL
FITNESS MONITOR

Pulse transmitter:

Length: 5½"
Width: 1⅕"
Thickness: ½"
Weight: 2 oz.

Wristwatch/receiver:

Length: 2"
Width: 1⅚"
Thickness: ⅝"
Weight: 2 oz.
Cost: $295

The Benchmark Quantum XL is the most comfortable heart-rate monitor I've ever used. Lightweight and small in size, it is nonetheless a heavyweight when it comes to performance. It's now an integral part of my training equipment. It combines a chest strap with carbon rubber electrodes and a snap-on transmitter that registers heart rate. This information is transmitted through the watery tissues of the body to the wristwatch/receiver, where the heart rate is displayed on the face of the watch.

Benchmark Quantum XL Fitness Monitor

   In addition to being able to continually monitor the heart rate during a workout, the memory function of the Quantum records and stores the pulse. When programmed, the pulse memory will recall pulse and the minute it was taken, thereby allowing post-training and rehabilitation analysis of heart-rate response.

Computer Instruments Corporation
100 Madison Ave.
Hempstead, NY 11550
(800) 227-1314

CIC DELUXE DIGITAL PULSEMETER
MODEL 8329

Length: 5"
Width: 2¾"
Thickness: 1¼"
Weight: 8 oz.
Cost: $159

This is a very dependable ear-lobe clip pulse meter that comes with a programmable high-rate alarm. When you leave the upper reaches of your target heart zone, colored lights flash and a beeper tone changes its pitch. Powered by four AA batteries, this model also gives elapsed time and current heartbeat (30 to 200 bpm) in an easy-to-read liquid crystal display (LCD) readout.

CIC Deluxe Digital Pulsemeter Model 8329

EXERSENTRY PULSEMINDER
MODEL EXIII

Length: 4"
Width: 2½"
Thickness: 1"
Weight: 3 oz.
Cost: $180

Here's the top of the line from CIC. The Exersentry provides accurate heart-rate monitoring with programmable high and low exercise target heart zones and alarms that ring when you're not exercising within these ranges. To use the unit, slip on the electrode chest strap, attach the lightweight monitor to the wire coming from the strap, and begin exercising. Simply by glancing at the pulse meter you will see your current pulse on the LCD screen.

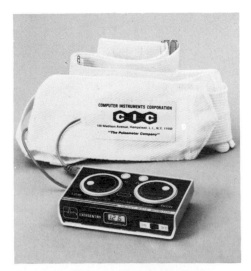

Exersentry Pulseminder Model EXIII

PART III

HOW TO HELP YOURSELF

TEN

WHERE TO SHOP FOR EQUIPMENT: ON BEING AN EDUCATED CONSUMER

WHEN DECIDING ON EQUIPMENT FOR YOUR HOME GYM, THE BEST thing to do is find a store that at least has the equipment on display. Then, put on some workout gear and go in and try the machines for yourself. This is the only sensible way to purchase home exercise equipment. If the salespeople don't let you try the equipment, you know you're in the wrong store.

If you choose to go to a department or discount store for your equipment, I think you're making a mistake. Yes, you will initially save some money, but chances are you might not get the best machine for you. Too often at a department store you will find that the equipment is improperly set up. At one large Florida department store I once saw a floor-model rower on display with the oars put on backward. The sad part is that they probably sold a few of these rowers to unsuspecting customers who then put their oars on backward.

If department store home exercise equipment doesn't work properly when you try it, don't be surprised. At one New York store I tried to change the speed on an expensive motorized treadmill, but it stayed locked in that one speed. So ended my trial run. Ever try to ride an exercise bike with only one pedal? That's the kind of bike a flustered salesman tried to sell me in a store in Boston.

If you insist on going to a department store for your exercise equipment, don't count on too much help from the salespeople. If you've read this far in the book, you probably know more about fitness and exercise equipment than most of the sales staff!

When buying home exercise equipment, I'm a great believer in the specialty fitness store. These stores provide three important services that you just don't find in any other kind of store.

1. *Selection.* Quality equipment manufacturers will sell only to specialty stores because they know that unlike the department stores, a specialty store will demonstrate the equipment, know its workings, and service it if and when it breaks. Also, at a good fitness store the consumer should be able to find a wide array of quality exercise machines at all the different price points.

At department stores you will find low-end to middle-range pieces of equipment. These machines often have the appearance of the much more expensive quality machines, but often fall far short on the performance end. The department store exercise machine may initially save you some money, but it's bound to make your inner fear of "Oh my God, I'll never use this" a self-fulfilling prophecy.

2. *Knowledgeable sales staff.* In a good fitness store you're likely to find sales help who will direct you to the right equipment for your needs. At the Concept 90 Fitness Stores, an East Coast home fitness chain based in Fort Lauderdale, Florida, sales personnel are required to take an intensive nine-day course in which they are instructed in the basics of fitness as well as the "how and why" of each piece of home exercise equipment.

"What we are selling at Concept 90 is physical fitness, not just home equipment," says Mike Shea, the CEO of Concept 90 and the mastermind behind the training course. "When the training course is over, what we have are educated and well-skilled exercise equipment salespeople. They now understand how a machine works, but more importantly how it can benefit the different customers that we deal with. It's better for us this way, and it's certainly better for the consumer."

3. *Set up, delivery, service.* Most home exercise machines are bulky, heavy, and come unassembled. A good fitness store will set up your exercise equipment, deliver it, and install it. Should something break or wear out on the machine, they'll service or replace it quickly. Very often, fixing a broken machine means just picking up a replacement part at the fitness store and doing the simple repair work yourself.

Try dealing with a department store about a broken exercise machine after the purchase and you'll often be directed to the manufacturer. Many phone calls and trips to the post office later you may finally get the replacement part you need. But by this time you will have missed so many workouts that your fitness level will have plummeted and you have to start working your way up again.

I've learned my lesson about home-equipment purchases the hard way. In the beginning I bought most of my equipment from the department store thinking I'd save some money. But, after having to replace too many pieces that were defective or just not working the way I expected them to, I've switched to shopping at the specialty store and buying reliable brand-name products. I've upgraded all of my existing home equipment, and now when I exercise I concentrate only on my exercise plan. Gone are the days when I had to worry about the machine working properly. Quality machines accommodate you as opposed to the other way around, and you get great workouts every time out.

ELEVEN

MASSAGE: IT FEELS GREAT TO BE KNEADED

WHETHER YOU'VE JUST FINISHED A 1-HOUR RUN ON YOUR TREAD-mill or a hard 20-minute piece on your rowing machine, there's nothing like treating yourself to a good relaxing massage to ward off potential muscle soreness or tendon injury. A massage will get your blood flowing, soothe your nerves, separate muscle fibers that have actually become stuck together during a hard workout, and help flush your system of waste matter. But, most of all, a massage will make you feel great.

"The most important benefit of massage," explains Bruria Ginton, RMT (registered massage therapist), former president of the New York Chapter of the American Massage Therapy Association, the professional association of qualified massage therapists, "is that massage helps increase your circulation while you are at rest. In the normal

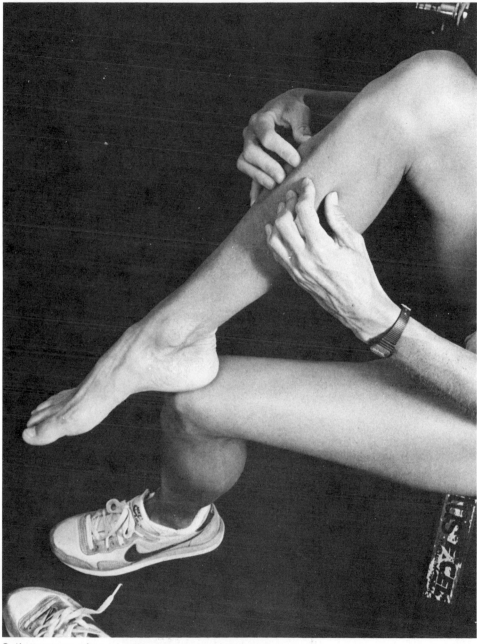

Self-massage after a workout helps you feel great.

metabolic process, the muscles have to receive certain amounts of nutrients to produce energy as well as get rid of the wastes produced as that energy is used and consumed. This way the body is kept in balance. Shortly after you finish exercising, though, the body is put out of balance. So you soon feel stiff and sore and become prone to injury. This is where massage can benefit an exerciser."

How Massage Works

Although massage has been with us since the time of the ancient Greeks, who used to carry around bottles of scented oil with them for their daily rub, not enough scientific studies have been undertaken to determine how and why massage benefits exercisers. The most widely accepted hypothesis is that chemical byproducts (lactic acid) created by an increased metabolic rate in the muscles accumulate and remain in the muscles instead of being eliminated through the bloodstream. Since exercise causes above-normal metabolic wastes, not enough of the waste products can be taken away by the blood as readily as desirable. It is these remaining lactates that cause the stiffness and pain that you feel after a workout and that hinder your movements, sometimes for days.

By massaging the body at rest, however, blood circulation is enhanced through dilation of the blood-carrying capillaries, speeding up the removal of toxins. This in turn allows you to come back to your next workout feeling refreshed and ready to go.

SELF-MASSAGE

When I was in college at Villanova, anyone who got a massage was considered a sissy. Even with all my international running and easy access to very good massage therapists in Europe especially, I avoided getting massages because of my subconscious idea that I would be a sissy if I did. It wasn't until the late 1970s that I overcame my hesitancy about massage. After a long and tiring transcontinental flight to attend a track meet, I let Frank Medina, the U.S. national track team trainer, give me a massage. I had to admit that I felt great afterward. I was relaxed, loose, and supple. The next night I set an American record in the 5,000-meter race. Frank turned into my secret training weapon, and for the rest of my active running career I always had him give me a massage when he was available.

Since leaving the running world I have been treated by massage therapists on a regular basis. I also use self-massage after many of my home workouts. Giving yourself a massage can never be as effective as getting one from a professional massage therapist. Since you are the source of the energy in self-massage, your body can never be totally relaxed—a major condition for optimum benefit. The body continues to work and to produce some elevations of wastes as you rub and stroke, thereby keeping you from getting the fullest benefit of massage.

This is not to say that self-massage is not worthwhile. Of course, you can't massage your back by yourself, an area so often in great need of massage, but you can effectively massage your knees, ankles, wrists, elbows, face, and, to some extent, shoulders. You can also massage your hands and feet, as well as the larger muscles of your calves, thighs (back and front), forearms, and upper arms (bicep and tricep). A good self-massage can prevent muscle and tendon injury by helping to increase blood flow and reduce the discomfort (stiffness) you feel in these areas after a workout.

Since you are the originator of the massage, as well as the beneficiary of it, one helpful aspect of self-massage is that you know how much pressure you can take on those tight or sore spots and can decide how long you want to massage yourself.

Technique

In self-massage the actual massage techniques are very easy to learn and will vary somewhat depending on the body area that you are working on. The postworkout massage technique most used will be the "friction" movement, a slow circular movement in which you press an area of flesh and gently squeeze and knead it either with your thumb or with your other four fingers (your thumb acting as an anchor). Apply gentle pressure at first, kneading the area in a circular motion, larger circles over muscle tissue and small circles over the bony tissue of the joints. Gradually increase pressure as you rub, but never beyond the point of pain. The purpose of friction is to mechanically loosen up stiff, tight, and congested areas.

Another very easy to learn and master self-massage stroke is the "modified effleurage." Here the purpose is to promote return of blood to veins. The direction of the massage strokes is toward the heart.

However, since you are both the operator as well as receiver in self-massage, instead of the normally practiced "pushing" effleurage technique, you will spread your fingers and perform an upward "pulling" motion in a rakelike manner. Pressure in this "modified effleurage" should be heavier than a pleasant tickle and always lighter than the pain threshold. The emphasis is on consistency and continuity.

The "pressure point" massage technique can be used throughout the body, but it is particularly recommended for areas that are rich in small bones, short muscles, and nerve endings. Here we are mainly dealing with the hands and feet, which, according to both Eastern and Western philosophies—yet to be scientifically proved—are areas that are reflective to the rest of the body. Working on these areas is assumed to relieve pain and congestion throughout the body.

"Pressure-point massage should be thought of as 'leaning point' massage," says Ginton, the founder and director of the Health Massage Group, New York's first professional massage group practice. "Unlike other types of massage, the effect of this movement is not the result of power and strength. Rather, it is a function of intention and timing."

In this "leaning point" massage you first inhale deeply, then with your thumb you lean into each point to be massaged *as you exhale.* This is very important, for it is your breathing that actually triggers the relaxation mechanism throughout the body. Your exhalation will actually facilitate your leaning with the proper slow, legato-like timing.

Rubbing Oils

"Just as a painter knows that he wants to get a certain consistency from his paints," says Ginton, "so too the massage therapist or someone giving himself a massage wants to get a certain consistency that will allow him to keep up the pressure on the body in a controlled and correct manner—a feel for the medium, here the muscle tissue. A good massage oil will allow you to do this."

Although you can use hand cream, baby oil, or even salad oil, the massage oils you can purchase in health-food stores or athletic outlets may actually be the best, because they're specially formulated to provide the right consistency. A good massage oil will have a pleasant fragrance, be easy to wipe off the body, and will leave the skin feeling refreshed and smooth. At present, an 8-ounce bottle will sell for $5 to $6, while a gallon costs about $35. "What some people like to do is mix their own oil," says David Simpson, a massage therapist at the Swedish Institute of Massage in New York City. "By adding vitamin E or almond extract to safflower oil, they can get both the consistency and the aroma that they want."

Self-Massage Tips

1.   To increase the blood supply to any area, it is not necessary to apply a lot of pressure in your massage strokes. Certainly, when in doubt, underpress rather than overpress.

2.   When massaging your large muscles, always stroke toward the heart. In this way you push the blood through the open "doors" of the veins, rather than applying pressure in the opposite direction and thus—always to be avoided—against the valves of the veins.

3.   If you have varicose veins in your legs, don't massage them.

4.   Whenever you feel as if you are coming down with a cold or flu *and* are running a fever, refrain from massage.

5.   If you have recently injured yourself and have some inflammation—for instance, a swollen joint—consult your physician before any massage.

6.   Don't ever feel guilty about giving yourself a massage or going for regular visits to a professional massage therapist. You've exercised, you've earned a massage! Finally, when used in conjunction with exercise and good nutrition, massage is a powerful tool to help you deal successfully with the stresses of everyday life.

Where to Massage

THE JOINTS

Your knees, ankles, shoulders, elbows, and wrists have less circulation than the rest of the body, so it's not uncommon to feel stiff and sore in any of these areas after you exercise. It's for this reason that massage here is very important. Good massage will help increase the flow of waste-carrying blood from the joints, which will help speed up recuperation and alleviate postworkout pain.

Begin by pouring a little massage oil on your palm, then rubbing your hands together to warm the liquid. Use a small, slow circular motion with the tip of your thumb (or other fingers), and gently move around the joint.

FEET AND HANDS

Start with the same pressure technique that you used on the joints, moving in a slow circular motion. Begin with light pressure and increase it gradually as you continue the massage.

MUSCLE TISSUE

Your success on your home gym equipment depends in great measure on effective blood circulation. In exercising, your muscles need to get nutrients as well as have waste products removed. Massage can be a positive factor because it increases blood flow at rest and thereby helps speed the flushing and cleansing function of the blood.

Apply the oil to your palms and spread your fingers wide. When possible, use both hands. Apply light and then increasing pressure to the muscle in a rakelike motion, as if you were raking leaves. Always "massage" toward the heart, though your hands remain in contact on each return stroke.

Consumer Tips

"A truly qualified professional massage therapist will have a professional working environment, and will ask questions about your medical history, specific muscle problems, diet, and exercise," says Ginton. "Most importantly, though, he or she will be responsible enough to refrain from massage when it's counterindicated, perhaps even to refer you to a physician, when necessary."

To help the consumer who is looking for a qualified massage therapist, Ginton offers the following advice.

- Always look for a state license and valid registration.
- Don't hesitate to ask the therapist about his or her training.
- Ask about related education.
- Ask about membership in the American Massage Therapy Association. (This is particularly important in states where a professional license is not yet required by law.)
- Beware of bargain offers. Depending upon experience, reputation of the therapist, and geographic location, prices range from $35 to $80 per hourly session.
- Look for professional affiliations with physicians and other health professionals.
- Beware of unrealistic promises, "health prophesies," and "cure-all" claims.

- Note whether a medical history is requested on your first visit. It should be.
- Note whether your therapist keeps a professional dress code.
- Expect to make an appointment rather than be a "walk-in."
- Ask yourself if the therapist is responsive to your feelings and needs; does he/she respond to feedback or offer professional explanation of his/her methods?

I've come 180 degrees in my thinking about massage therapy since my college days and am now a firm believer in the healthful benefits of massage. If only once in your life, try a massage in the hands of a professional massage therapist and I'm sure you'll become like me, a believer. You'll also learn firsthand how to perform the proper strokes and how much pressure can be applied to your muscles. Hopefully, once at home you'll be able to duplicate many of these strokes on yourself. Returning to the massage therapist for refresher courses a few times a year is something that I like to do, a special treat that I reward myself with after a series of particularly good workouts. It's a great incentive for a home workout!

Personal trainers can provide instruction, encouragement, and inspiration. Bruce Baltz (center) assists two of his clients in a home workout. Photo credit: Yuka Kawachi

TWELVE

DO YOU NEED A PERSONAL TRAINER?

DO YOU LACK THE SELF-MOTIVATION TO WORK OUT AT HOME, OR do you just need someone to show you how to get the most out of your home equipment? A good solution to your workout blues just might be a personal trainer.

A personal trainer is that well-conditioned person who arrives at a home, gym bag in hand, and stands by to give one-to-one instruction, helpful tips, and plenty of motivation as the client goes through a complete home gym workout. Under their trainer's watchful eye, many home exercisers sweat and strain to finish their workouts—workouts that most exercisers never would have completed if left to their own devices. For this service most personal trainers get paid anywhere from $40 to $100 an hour.

Anyone can call himself or herself a personal trainer; there are no national licensing or certification boards for these exercise vagabonds. Some have college degrees in physical education, while others just like

205

to work out and are either spirited enough or talented enough to get the weak of body doing it as well. In any large American city a good trainer will have a large and loyal following because he or she can guarantee the bottom line for his clients: physical fitness.

With so many people locked into the fast lane at the office, waiting in line at the health club in order to exercise is certainly a waste of time and is no longer acceptable. Having home equipment but never using it is just as bad. But now, by simply penciling in an appointment with a home trainer, busy and once-unmotivated Americans are now exercising regularly with someone who will come to their home regularly to monitor, coach, and cajole them through sound and structured exercise programs.

"Even if they have the latest equipment, many people don't know what to do when they exercise by themselves," says Bruce Baltz, a New York City–based personal trainer whose client list includes well-known celebrities from TV and movies, business execs, dancers, and marathon runners, as well as arthritics and the blind. Baltz, who worked as a trainer at New York's Sports Training Institute before branching out on his own, generally begins work at 6:30 A.M. and finishes at 9:00 P.M. Most of his male clients want to work on their midsections, while the women are concerned mostly with their thighs and hips.

"Many of my clients were unsure if they were pushing themselves hard enough in their workouts when they were exercising by themselves," says Baltz. "And most of the time they weren't. What's different now for them is that I not only show them how to exercise, but I'm there to encourage that little something extra out of them as they exercise. It makes a big difference."

For some, perhaps, having a personal trainer show up at the door may be nothing more than the latest status symbol. But if you seriously want to have an in-house coach to guide and motivate you to fitness, and to give you knowledge that will last a lifetime, a good personal trainer can't be beat. The hardest part, though, is finding a good trainer.

"I think the easiest way to go about it," says Baltz, "is to contact the director of a good health club in your area. Another way is to call the beauty editor of your local magazine or newspaper. These people generally have a good idea of who's available and how to contact them."

Once you have found a trainer, there are several things you should ask during your initial interview. Can the trainer help design a program around your present home gym equipment? Does he stress aerobic exercise, strength training, or a mixture of the two? If you're interested in preparing for an upcoming sports season, will this trainer be able to design a program to help you get in good physical shape?

If you really want a personal trainer but a particular trainer's philosophy and program doesn't agree with the one that *you* want, or if his or her personality is too much like a drill sergeant's for your taste, then by all means continue elsewhere with your search. With some time, patience, and effort you'll eventually come up with someone who will not only be able to show you how to make the most of your exercise time but, more important, how to achieve and maintain fitness.

THIRTEEN

INJURIES: THE COMMON ACHES AND PAINS

EXERCISE IS A TYPE OF BODY STRESS. IF THE EXERCISE OR MOVE-ment isn't properly performed, or if it's performed too intensely, it will do more harm than good. Injuries—the aches and pains, muscle tears, and sprains—are something that you can expect at one time or another during the course of your home workouts. This chapter will help you to better understand how your body-machine works, what you can do to prevent yourself from getting injured during a home workout, how you can best be treated when you are injured, and when it's time for you to cut back on your exercise program because of an injury.

Lower-Back Pain

Lower-back pain can bring even the most serious home exercise program to a sudden halt and keep it shut down for quite some time as you undergo rehabilitation. According to Dr. Jay Okin, a New York City chiropractor who has many professional ballerinas as patients, lower-back pain manifests itself through one or several of the following forms: severe pain in the lower back or buttocks, with shooting pains going down the legs; an inability to straighten up without holding on to something for support; muscle spasms that cause you to actually tilt to one side; disc protrusion; muscle imbalance.

The statistics on lower-back pain are staggering:

- It affects 80 percent of Americans at some time in their life; 74 million are afflicted annually.
- 2.5 million are totally disabled by the pain.
- It's the number-two cause of work loss, costing American employers $20–$30 billion yearly.
- It causes 65 million doctor visits annually, costing patients $5 billion.
- It's the number-one complaint treated by orthopedists.

The exact causes of lower-back pain are varied. Poor posture, improper lifting (as in lifting free weights, your child, or even a bag of groceries), or a physical trauma or sudden twisting or rotation of the lower back (bouncing or jerking in a warm-up exercise) are some of the causes.

If you suffer lower-back pain while exercising, stop exercising immediately. Don't be foolish and think you can work through the pain. Rest is very important. Don't begin exercise or any physical work until you are pain free. Otherwise, you'll aggravate and therefore prolong your condition. If the pain does clear up within a few days and you have sufficient muscle strength, start light strengthening exercises for your back and abdomen.

If the pain doesn't go away in a few days, seek professional help from your doctor, orthopedist, or chiropractor.

In mild cases the treatment of lower-back pain may require nothing more than rest, aspirin, and special exercises. The more-serious cases may necessitate a visit to either a chiropractor, who will take X-rays and then manipulate the spine to relieve the pressure on the spinal nerves, or to an orthopedist, who will take X-rays, prescribe muscle relaxants, or prescribe orthotics to stabilize any imbalance that's found.

Once back pain is relieved, the patient is recovered. But never completely cured. Once you have lower-back pain you'll be a candidate for it for the rest of your life. Lower-back exercises must be done daily to maintain strength and balance in both your abdomen (your stomach muscles support your pelvis) and pelvic region. Strong stomach and back muscles will greatly reduce pressure on your spinal column and keep you relatively injury free.

Whether or not you have ever suffered the most unpleasant experience of lower-back pain, here are some ways to ensure that you keep standing tall.

- Keep your weight down. Being overweight taxes both the stomach and the back muscles.
- Sleep on the firmest mattress possible. This will support your spine and keep it aligned.
- When lifting heavy objects, squat down and lift with the force coming from your legs and thighs—not from your back. Never lift a heavy object higher than your waist.
- Use a rocking chair. This will rest your back muscles.
- After you awaken, perform your lower-back exercises to loosen and stretch your back. Perform them once again before you begin your home exercise program. Shortened, improperly stretched muscles can quickly lead to lower-back problems by causing a severe muscle imbalance that will ultimately overtax the back.
- When running, cycling, skipping, or rowing at home, avoid any abrupt change in your tempo or pace. Always move into sprint work gradually and with a proper warm-up behind you.
- Avoid jerking or twisting your back in weight training. Wear a weight belt for support whenever you are lifting heavy loads.

The Muscles

The human body is composed of more than four hundred muscles that allow you to walk, run, bend over, even blink your eyes. Whenever muscles shorten, the tendons located at the end of the muscle pull on your bones and allow you to perform the desired action.

PULLED MUSCLE

A muscle pull, or strained muscle as it's sometimes called, is a tender and sometimes painful tear, an overstretching, or an actual rip of the muscle. Often it comes on without warning. A muscle pull is very often accompanied by spasms, bruising, or swelling. In the more severe cases, a snapping sound is heard as the muscle fibers tear away from the muscle. On the other hand, a chronic muscle pull is characterized as one that comes on slowly with a dull ache and stays for quite some time before it is healed.

Muscle pulls are usually caused by overworking them. Improper warm-ups, overstretching, sudden accelerations, slowing down too quickly, or direct blows to the muscle group will also bring on a muscle injury.

The first phase of treatment for any muscle pull is RICE, an acronym for rest, ice, compression, and elevation (see p. 215). This is followed by light stretching exercises once the pain has stopped or lessened. In some cases this could be days later. In the case of a muscle injury accompanied by swelling and a lot of pain, a visit to the doctor for treatment and a prescribed rehabilitation program is in order.

MUSCLE CRAMP

A cramp is a painful spasm of a muscle. The pain can last anywhere from a few seconds to a few hours. Cramps are generally caused by one of the following:

- overexercise
- excessive loss of body minerals such as sodium, magnesium, or potassium during home exercise
- an accumulation of lactic acid in a muscle group
- dehydration
- a slight muscle strain

Treatment for cramps includes immediate massage and stretching of the cramped muscle. In some cases RICE may be necessary. To prevent cramping, always make sure that you drink a few glasses of water before you begin exercising, and a few more glasses every 15 minutes as you exercise. During heavy exercise bouts the body loses tremendous amounts of fluid in the form of sweat and vapor from your mouth. You will lose even more if the room is poorly ventilated.

MUSCLE SORENESS

Everyone experiences some muscle soreness, from the highly trained athlete to the out-of-condition weekend warrior who's just starting a home exercise program. It's not uncommon for veteran exercisers to experience sore muscles during a workout or to have the soreness mysteriously come on one or two days after the workout. The causes and cures of muscle soreness, like the common cold, still remain a medical mystery. Researchers do have some theories about muscle soreness, but nothing is conclusive.

There are two types of muscle soreness. Acute muscle soreness is what you often feel while lifting weights or using some form of resistance machine such as a rower. The exercised muscle group starts to ache and you stop exercising because of the pain that you experience. Shortly after you stop exercising, the pain diminishes and soon disappears.

Researchers believe that this particular muscle soreness is caused by ischemia, or inadequate blood flow. Scientists theorize that when you lift weights or pull or push hard against resistance on your exercise machine, you are actually reducing the flow of blood to the muscles. This causes the muscles to constrict, which can cause pain and can also reduce the blood's function of "cleaning out" metabolic byproducts from your working muscles. This lactate residue clogging the muscles is another reason for the pain you feel.

Delayed muscle soreness is the second type of soreness, and it usually sets in anywhere from 24 to 48 hours after you have finished exercising. Scientists are in agreement that exercise, with all of its muscular contractions, actually damages the muscle fibers and connective tissue to some extent. This damage then causes the muscles to swell. Sensitive nerve endings are then stimulated and this results in the feeling of muscle soreness.

All exercisers are equally susceptible to delayed muscle soreness. Accelerating your training too quickly, using different muscle groups to perform a task, or putting too much stress on the body through interval work will very often bring on delayed muscle soreness. These muscle aches are not harmful to you in any way and will disappear in a few days.

TREATMENT FOR MUSCLE SORENESS

There is no effective medical treatment for muscle soreness. The following remedies will alleviate the pain and diminish the symptoms of muscle soreness:

- massage
- aspirin
- heat treatments
- liniments containing wintergreen oil
- light stretching routines
- light exercise

When you have extreme muscle soreness, don't try to work through the pain; you will only aggravate the situation. If muscle pain or cramping persists for more than a week, contact your physician.

HOW TO PREVENT MUSCLE SORENESS

Although everyone is susceptible to muscle soreness, here are some tips that may help you avoid the aches and pains.

- When you are just beginning a weight-training program or are beginning to work out on a new piece of exercise equipment, always start with weights, repetitions, or allotted times that are much lower and lighter than recommended. Gradually introduce your body to increased weight or new resistances over a period of time.
- Before you begin to exercise hard, make sure that your muscles are warm and ready for the upcoming stress. A good sign of being properly warmed up is if you are sweating slightly. When the workout is over, cool down for at least 5 minutes before ending your workout. This gradual reduction of exercise intensity will greatly aid in the prevention of muscle soreness.
- Never bounce or jerk your muscles in any exercise movement. This can easily tear or unnaturally push the muscles past their normal length. Injury will result.

The Joints

A body joint is simply a hinge, a junction where two bones meet. Cartilage, a durable milky-white covering, lines the ends of the bones and keeps them from rubbing roughly against each other. Cartilage does not have its own blood supply and can't repair itself if it becomes chipped or torn. Another worrisome aspect of cartilage is that it can become worn down from overuse or abuse. Riding an improperly fitted stationary bike, for example, can cause your knees and the cartilage surrounding them to sustain tremendous force. The end result could be cartilage damage if you continue to exercise for prolonged periods.

Proper exercise is good for your cartilage, greatly increasing its thickness and thereby providing more protection for your joints. Merely warming up prior to exercise is enough to cause the cartilage to temporarily swell and thicken. You can easily understand the problems caused if you warm up improperly or skip a warm-up entirely. If too much stress is then placed on a "cold" joint in the course of your exercise, cartilage may actually be sheared off due to the extreme force placed on the joint. Surgery is often needed to remove the loose piece of cartilage.

The knee, hip, ankle, elbow, shoulder, and wrist joints are the joints continuously used in exercise. All injuries to your joints, whether from twisting, overuse, or a sharp blow, can knock you out of training for a long time. Whatever you do, don't disregard joint pain and try to "train through it." Once you notice any pain in your joints, start RICE treatment. If pain persists, consult your physician.

Ligaments

Ligaments are sturdy bands of fiber that attach near the ends of bones where the joints are formed. Their function is to add stability to the joint by holding the bones together when the joint moves. Although the ligaments are fairly strong and flexible, it's possible to stretch, sprain, or tear them by a sudden jerking or twisting of a joint area. A stretched ligament, given proper rest, will regain its former length. For lesser ligament injuries, RICE is often successfully used in rehabilitation. However, more serious ligament injuries often require surgery. Consult your physician.

Tendons

Tendons are extensions of the muscles and help attach the muscles to bone. Tendonitis—an inflammation or irritation of the tendon—will cause the tendon to swell abnormally and bring on pain or stiffness. Tendonitis is sometimes distinguished by the slight grinding noise you hear as you move the injured part through its range of motion. The condition is brought on by tight, improperly stretched and warmed up muscles, as well as from general overstress caused by too much exercising.

TREATMENT

- Stop all hard exercise once soreness develops.
- When the pain and soreness stops, start stretching exercises to reduce tendon pressure and prevent recurrences.

RICE

Many injuries that you will receive during the course of exercising will be minor and will not require a visit to the doctor. By understanding RICE—rest, ice, compression, elevation—one of the basic principles of injury rehabilitation, you will speed up your recovery from injury, whether it be from an ankle sprain, a simple muscle pull, or a broken leg.

When an injury occurs from working out at home, start RICE treatments immediately to counteract the effects of swelling. Continue the treatment for up to three days.

Heat, whether a hot bath, whirlpool, or heating pad, should be started *only* when the swelling has gone down.This generally is 48 to 72 hours after the injury occurs. Heat increases blood flow to the injured area and causes it to swell, the main reason why it should not be applied right after an injury.

Rest

Once you feel pain, stop exercising. Rest prevents further aggravation of your injury.

Ice

Ice constricts the blood vessels and slows the supply of blood to the injured part. The more blood in the injured part, the longer it will take you to heal. Ice also reduces swelling, a major cause of pain (see Cryotherapy, p. 216).

Compression

Using an elastic support bandage is one of the best ways to inhibit swelling by pushing blood and fluids away from an injured area.

Elevation

By keeping the injured part above your heart level, you let gravitational forces drain excess fluids away from your injury, speeding up recovery by reducing the swelling.

Cryotherapy

Cryotherapy, the use of ice in the treatment of sprained ligaments, bruises, and muscle strains and pulls, is very popular today among leading athletic trainers and sportsmedicine physicians. Since the healing time after an injury is directly related to the time it takes to reduce the swelling, cryotherapy plays a critical role in quick and successful rehabilitation.

The chief benefit of treating your injury or soreness with ice is that ice dulls pain. It also reduces inflammation by causing the blood vessels to constrict, thereby cutting down the normal supply of blood and reducing the oxygen needs of the damaged tissue. Another benefit is that ice also dulls the nerve endings, interrupting the pain messages that are normally sent to the brain in time of an accident.

Caution is advised whenever you use ice therapy. Apply the ice no longer than 20 minutes or until your skin starts to feel numb—which can occur in as little as 10 minutes.

CRYOTHERAPY TECHNIQUES

Ice bag. Use an ice pack filled with crushed ice or cubes. Place the bag over a towel and apply to the injured area. If possible, hold the pack in place with an Ace bandage to provide compression and stability.
Ice bath. Immerse the injured part in a suitable container, or fill your tub with ice water. Keep the injured part immersed for as long as you can comfortably withstand but no longer than 20 minutes.
Ice therapy. Under the supervision of a doctor, trainer, or physical therapist, numb the injured part with ice applications or an ice bath.

Begin to move the injured part through its normal range of motion. This arctic treatment is often used with great success by sports trainers and is the best technique for speeding up healing and reducing rehabilitation time.

Ice massage. This is the safest and easiest-to-use cryotherapy technique and is especially good after a workout for treating minor aches and pains. To make your ice applicator, simply freeze water in a Styrofoam cup. When needed, peel off some of the side to expose the ice, then apply it to your skin in a circular motion. Use comfort as your guide in deciding how long to continue with the treatment. The small area you're working on initially should feel like it's "burning." It will then start to ache and finally will feel numb. For particularly tender spots, repeat the process a few times during the day.

See Your Doctor If . . .

Home treatment of your sports injuries has its place, but there may come a time when you need expert medical care. Go see your doctor if:

1.   You suffer an injury accompanied by severe pain and swelling.
2.   You have persistent ache in any of your joints that doesn't clear up after two weeks; or a dull pronounced joint pain that comes on once you begin to exercise. In many of these cases rest is all that is needed, but to be sure, check with your physician first before you aggravate the condition.
3.   You have an injury or pain that you're worried about and feel should be checked by your doctor.

What's Up, Doc?

If you exercise regularly you may work a muscle or tendon too hard, or just overwork one muscle group at the expense of another, which will then lead to imbalance. This can set off a whole series of potential chronic medical problems that will only become worse the longer you continue to exercise without seeking treatment.

The person who treats your injury will play an important part in how successfully the cause (not the symptom) of your problem is discovered and then eliminated. In choosing your physician, don't just flip through the Yellow Pages and then randomly select someone. I have had my share of doctor visits over the years, and what I now always recommend to my athletic friends when they're injured is that they look for a sportsmedicine physician. This is a doctor who is an expert in treating sports-related injuries. In addition to being a medical practitioner, a sports doc is generally an athlete (or at least an athlete at heart), and knows what stresses the body goes through in exercise because of his own athletic background.

A sportsmedicine doctor knows that it takes more than "take two aspirin and call me in the morning" to keep athletes moving and in good health. What a good sports doctor will do with you on your first visit is go through your training program with you, asking about your equipment and the various exercises that you do and the techniques that you use when performing them. This medical detective work allows your injury and its exact cause to be precisely diagnosed, and you'll be back to exercising as soon as possible.

Unfortunately, all doctors are not "created" equal. As Len Preheim of the Toga Bike Shop in New York always says when I bring up the subject of doctors: "The one who graduates at the bottom of the class of the lowliest medical school in the country is still called 'doctor.'" Preheim's message is clear. You have to use care and discretion in selecting your physician. Check with friends for their recommendations. Contact your local medical board or call a medical school in your area for their recommendations of sportsmedicine physicians.

Who's Who: A Look at Your Medical Options

ORTHOPEDIST (Medical Doctor, M.D.)

An orthopedist is a surgeon/physician who specializes in the musculo-skeletal system of the body; he treats fractures, aches, and pains, and prescribes medicine.

PODIATRIST (Doctor of Podiatric Medicine, D.P.M.)

A podiatrist is a specialist in the foot and all of its injuries, as well as injuries that imbalanced feet cause to the back, hips, or legs. In some states podiatrists may operate surgically on the ankle region and below. In an effort to alleviate knee, foot, hip, or back pain, podiatrists will often prescribe orthotics (custom-made leather or plastic inserts) that are worn in the shoes.

CHIROPRACTOR (Doctor of Chiropractic, D.C.)

A chiropractor treats weaknesses of the body through adjustments, an actual manipulation of the spinal column. Many chiropractors believe that all injuries and diseases are caused by misalignment of the vertebrae, which then disturbs nerve energy flow. Chiropractors will often recommend orthotics or other types of shoe inserts to relieve skeletal imbalances.

PHYSICAL THERAPIST (Registered Physical Therapist, R.P.T.)

A physical therapist uses manipulation, exercise programs, massage, and other treatments to restore biomechanical function.

ACUPUNCTURIST

An acupuncturist pierces nerves with needles to ease pain and bring about healing (an ancient Chinese therapy).

Alternatives to Maintaining Fitness When Injured

Very often, when you suffer an injury you may be temporarily prevented from continuing your normal exercise routine. In order to slow down the de-training effects that are associated with a reduction in exercise frequency, duration, and intensity, you should have an alternative exercise plan to carry you through until you recover. In order to be effective, this new or modified exercise program should involve your large muscle groups and be able to raise your heart rate up to your target heart zone.

If you have suffered a leg injury and can't run, a rowing machine or exercise bike might suit your exercise needs. If the injury is to your shoulders or arms, a bicycle or treadmill could be substituted to provide you with suitable exercise.

At some point, however, your injury may be such that home exercise is temporarily impossible. A swimming program may be a possible alternative. Swimming is a completely aerobic exercise that makes use of all muscle groups and at the same time puts very little stress on the muscles because the body is completely supported by water as you exercise. If you know the proper swim-stroke mechanics, you will very easily be able to work within your target heart zone for longer periods of time than you could with land-based exercise. Of course, if you don't have access to a pool, the major disadvantage of swimming is that your training may be too sporadic to be of any sustained cardiovascular benefit. Then, too, if you don't know how to swim properly, you will become exhausted too quickly in the water to achieve any real aerobic benefits.

In this country there are more than 4.5 million pools, 38,000 swimming clubs, and 2,600 swimming coaches. The nearest pool may be just a short distance from your home, and as you read this the local Masters swim club may be going through a workout. Masters Swimming is a nationwide program started in 1970 to provide pool time, coaching, competition, and camaraderie for those who want to achieve fitness through swimming. Many of the participants in the program are beginners, while others have competed for college swim teams or in the Olympic Games. Whatever your ability level, there's a spot for you in Masters Swimming. All you need is desire. To find out about joining a Masters club in your area, write:

U.S. Masters Swimming, Inc.
Dorothy Donnelly, Secretary
5 Pigott Lane
Avon, CT 06001

Enclose SASE

Afterword

I ENJOY WORKING OUT AT HOME. OFTEN MY NONEXERCISING friends will ask what kind of pleasure I can get from working out in a room—most of the time alone—and pushing myself and my heart to such high levels.

My reply to them is that exercising as I do helps to keep me fit. Although I am a competitive person, I am not competing against anyone in these home workouts. I have my own personal goals that I want to achieve, however. Being able to exercise indoors whenever I want and in any manner that I choose is now, for me, one of life's joys.

In my workout room I set my own goals, accept my own challenges. When I step into the room, my cares and problems of the day are left at the door. The time that I spend exercising energizes me. It gives me a great sense of well-being and accomplishment. And when it's all over, I feel better for having exercised. I can think and perform better at everything that awaits me. I am fit and I look forward to my next home workout.